sona
BOOKS

First published in the UK 2020 by Sona Books
an imprint of Danann Publishing Ltd.

All Images courtesy of Getty Images and;
Library of Congress, Minnesota Historical Society, NARA, Aaron Muszalski, Alamy, Ann Harkness,
Citizen University, Jamelle Bouie, The All-Nite Images, The Laura Flanders Show, RM Hermen,
US Information Agency, Corbis, Bettmann/Corbis Adrian Mann, Adam Jones Ph.D, City of
Birmingham Police Department Alabama, LBJ Foundation, CE Watkin, Richard Apple

Copy Editor Tom O'Neil
Redesign by Darren Grice @ Ctrl-D

CAT NO: **SON0483**
ISBN: **978-1-912918-31-7**

Made in EU.

THE HISTORY OF

THE CIVIL RIGHTS MOVEMENT

CONTENTS

WE SHALL OVERCOME

JIM CROW.

NEW YORK.

HERE LIES JIM CROW

1 January 1863

THE EMANCIPATION PROCLAMATION

The Emancipation Proclamation freed 3.1 million of the nation's four million slaves when it came into effect

President Abraham Lincoln's first reading of the Emancipation Proclamation, 22 July 1862, as shown in an engraving by Alexander Hay Ritchie dated 1866

Since 1619, slavery had cemented itself firmly into the culture and society of the New World and the United States of America it would become. It drove both trade and industry and had, quite literally, shaped the nation. It became embedded in normality so deeply that for many, enforced labour was as pedestrian as attending church on Sunday. But not everyone accepted its presence, including Abraham Lincoln, the 16th president of the United States and the man at the helm of government while the Civil War raged across the nation.

Lincoln had long been disgusted by slavery, but he knew that its deep integration in both the North and the South would make it an unwise avenue to pursue during wartime. However, that all changed by mid-1862, when thousands of slaves rebelled against their Southern masters and fled to join the invading armies of the Union. With this massive influx of humanity, Lincoln was now in a position to use the abolition of slavery as an acceptable war measure. And while a great many Republicans were opposed to any form of amendment to slavery law, it became clear that the vast majority of slaveholders were based in the South and that the war on them had become a de facto war on slavery itself.

The Proclamation itself wasn't the death of slavery – in fact, it was both a tactical manipulation of the law designed to undermine the South, and the first step towards systematically dismantling slavery in the United States. The new law granted freedom to all slaves rebelling against their masters in the South, but did not affect those owned in the North. It granted them the right to fight with the Union in the war, but did not grant them rights as citizens. It was a half-step for civil rights, but it was progress in the right direction nonetheless.

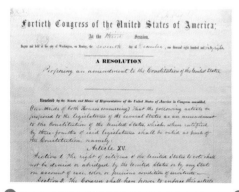

The 14th and 15th Amendments 9 July 1868
The 14th and 15th Amendments were, much like the 13th Amendment that preceded them, designed to bolster the basic principles of the Emancipation Proclamation. The 14th – brought into effect on 9 July 1868 - created protection for the civil rights of former slaves, while the 15th removed lawful limitations that stopped African American men from voting.

NAACP founded 12 February 1909
Formed over a century ago, the National Association for the Advancement of Colored People was created to fight, to rewrite, and to protect the civil rights of African Americans. The group was the successor to the Niagara Movement, which convened in Canada to discuss the growth of Jim Crow laws and the continued disenfranchisement of citizens of colour.

The Great Migration 1916
Between 1916 and 1970, over six million African Americans moved from their rural setting in the South to areas in the West, Midwest and Northeast of the United States. This incredible exodus was in reaction to multiple factors, including the rise of Jim Crow laws and violence against people of colour, as well as the impact of the Great Depression on rural-based communities.

DEFINING MOMENTS
1600S-1950S

ORIGINS

The Civil War begins
12 April 1861

Second Confiscation Act comes into effect
6 August 1861

Lincoln threatens South with the Proclamation
5 October 1953

LEGACY

Civil War comes to an end,
May 1865

13th Amendment protects slave freedoms
18 December 1865

14th Amendment guaranteed freed slave rights
9 July 1868

• Double V strategy
7 February 1942

During World War II, over 2.5 million African American men registered to fight. They served in every type of military corps, but experienced just as much alienation and segregation as life pre-war. The number of African American men enlisting rose significantly following the NAACP-sponsored recruitment campaign, known as the Double V strategy, which represented victory at home against the evil of racism, as well as victory abroad.

• Signing of Jackie Robinson
15 April 1947

In 1947, the Brooklyn Dodgers paved the way for sports in the US when it broke the 'colour line' of baseball by choosing to start second baseman, Jackie Robinson. By doing so, Robinson became the first ever officially recognised African American player in the MLB (Major League Baseball), and opened the gates for players of colour in all professional US sports.

• Executive Order 9981
26 July 1948

Back in 1948, then-president Harry S. Truman enacted Executive Order 9981, which effectively abolished racial segregation in all branches of the United States Armed Forces. It was designed to create military units comprising all races and religions, as well as opening up the right for any individual to enlist for military service in the United States.

AMERICA'S CENTURIES OF SLAVERY

America was founded on the principle of liberty and justice for all, but it wasn't the land of the free for everybody

America didn't invent slavery, but it embraced it with horrible enthusiasm. Slaves were the backbone of the American economy. Between 1790 and 1860 the harvesting of cotton in the Southern states grew from a thousand tons a year to a million, with slaves the crucial labour force needed to bring in those crops. In 1790 there were half a million slaves in the South. There were four million by 1860. The system was backed by legislation, the courts, the military and the government. The importation of slaves actually became illegal in 1808, but the law went unenforced, meaning that hundreds of thousands of slaves continued to be brought into the country, usually from Central and Western Africa. The system was so entrenched that only the Civil War could bring it to an end.

Slaves had a low life expectancy and were treated more like cattle than human beings; they were sold at auctions, where their physical attributes and talents were talked up as their most marketable qualities. Slave owners would often break up families, selling husbands or wives, or their children. This was often a deliberate policy to subdue the slaves' spirits - after all, a slave without a family was thought to have less will to resist. There were also sometimes economic reasons: at one point there was such a surplus of slave labour in the Upper South that a forced migration of more than a million slaves to the Deep South was implemented. Through all of this, slaves held on to their humanity. Torn from their families, they formed deep kinships with their companions on the plantations. Music, dancing, art and religion all remained important - although the latter could be used against the slaves. Black preachers were also sometimes employed to preach in ways that kept the slaves in line.

Whippings and other brutal punishments were not only widespread but normal. Slave revolts were unusual since they were swiftly put down with military force. Escape was more common, although risky. Successful runaways made new lives in Canada, Mexico or the North, but getting caught in the process of escape meant getting torn apart by dogs, or shot. The Fugitive Slave Act was passed in 1850 to make it easier for slave owners to reclaim their 'property' south of the border in Mexico, and there were laws to dissuade white people from giving aid to escaped slaves. Poor, uneducated white people were employed as overseers of black labour, entrenching white racism in the South for decades to come.

> **Slaves in Kentucky in the 1860s were valued between $40 to $400 each. Strong males in their 20s were highly prized**

Unsurprisingly there were uprisings, although most were swiftly crushed. One of the most famous was led by Nat Turner on 21 August 1831. Turner and his band of brothers were ultimately unsuccessful, and security in the South became even tighter as a result of their rebellion. But the voices of abolitionists were getting louder. In 1853, John Brown (a white man) hatched a plan to seize the federal arsenal at Harper's Ferry, Virginia and spark a slave revolt throughout the South. Local militia, plus hundreds of marines under the command of General Robert E Lee, put down the insurgency (Brown was hanged), but it was clear that the issue was far from concluded. Still, as late as 1857 the supreme court ruled that Dred Scott could not sue for his freedom because he was property and not legally a person.

All of the above took place under the presidency of Andrew Jackson. Abraham Lincoln replaced him in 1860, with discomfort about slavery part

Robert E Lee, the commander of the defeated Confederate States Army

Slave market, Richmond,
Virginia 1853

Union Army general Ulysses S Grant became president in 1869 and worked to protect the civil rights of former slaves

Slaves were the most valuable asset of the American economy, worth roughly $3 billion in 1860

of his platform (though he wasn't strictly abolitionist). The secession from the Union of 11 pro-slavery Confederate states reliant on slave labour for the plantation system took place the same year. Lincoln began leaning politically slightly further to the left thanks to the continuing pressure of abolitionists.

Congress passed the Emancipation Proclamation, declaring slaves on all Confederate territory immediately free, in 1862, although the North was hardly a utopia of equality: citizens were still allowed to own slaves as long as they were loyal to the United States. Lincoln argued passionately about the humanitarian wrongness of slavery (although he was careful not to advocate any sort of social or political equality between white and black). By the summer of 1864, buoyed by the Emancipation Proclamation, anti-slavery petitioners had sent 400,000 signatures to Congress demanding slavery be abolished. The Senate and the House of Representatives signed off on the 13th Amendment to the US Constitution. Slavery was legally over.

While the government could legislate against slavery, however, it could hardly legislate against racism. With the Civil War now regarded to a great extent as one of black liberation, the resentment of white people drafted to fight in it became dangerously volatile (especially since the draftees were usually poor – whites with money could buy their way out of fighting). There were draft riots, in which cities were overrun with anti-black violence. But the African Americans in the South now found themselves with unexpected power, since the Confederacy, perversely, needed them to fight the Union. It could either free its slaves, enlist them in its army and use them to fight in the war – thereby negating the point of much of the conflict – or it could refuse and watch its enslaved workforce down tools and defect to the Union Army. Congress granted equal pay to black and white soldiers in April 1864. A year later, with the Confederate troops depleted and demoralised, the war was finally over. Lee surrendered to Grant.

Despite the new rights of freed African Americans to vote, be educated and serve politically, however, white American society, especially in the South, remained aggressively opposed to equal rights for black people. President Andrew Johnson, who took office after Lincoln's assassination, was firmly on the side of the whites on these issues, refusing legislation leaning towards racial equality. Slavery may have been over, and black children attending school, but former slaves found themselves living and working on the same plantations, unable, both financially and legally, to buy or rent their own land, and forced to work under strict labour contracts with prison sentences the punishment for breaking them. These were the Black Codes that formed the antecedents of the 'Jim Crow' segregationist laws of the 20th century.

Black votes played a huge part in the election of President Ulysses S Grant in 1869, and with Johnson out of the picture, some societal progress was made, with equality laws passed and constitutional amendments put forward.

But whenever the cause of African American rights advanced, there was white resistance to meet it. Racist groups like the Ku Klux Klan sprang up to terrorise black people and keep them oppressed, and as those groups gained more and more members, politicians desperate for votes were forced to pander to them. The African American blacksmith Charles Caldwell shot a white attacker in self-defence and was acquitted of murder at the subsequent trial. He was the first black man ever to kill a white man in Mississippi and go free. Not long afterwards, however, he was murdered by a white gang. The white South was going to continue to make its own justice, regardless of laws that suggested otherwise.

NAT TURNER'S SLAVE REBELLION

Nat Turner lived his entire life in Southampton County, Virginia. Intelligent and religiously devout, he could read and write at an early age and, by his twenties, he was preaching services to his fellow slaves. He became known locally as 'The Prophet' for that reason, and because of the spiritual visions he claimed to have. One such vision in 1828, when Turner was 28, inspired him to begin planning a violent uprising, which finally took place in August 1831. Turner interpreted a solar eclipse on the 13th of the month as a sign from God for the slaves to begin the fight back against their oppression.

Having banded together a force of about 70 men, Turner began travelling from house to house in Southampton County, freeing slaves and killing their white 'masters'. The murder was indiscriminate, including women and children, and Turner and his rebels were responsible for at least 60 deaths before they were stopped, finally overwhelmed by a white militia with more than double the manpower of the insurrectionists. The uprising had lasted two days.

Over 50 black men and women were executed in the aftermath on charges of murder, conspiracy and treason. Turner himself was hanged on 11 November, and his corpse flayed, decapitated and dismembered. The following year in Virginia, it became illegal for slaves to be educated, or to hold religious meetings in the absence of a white minister.

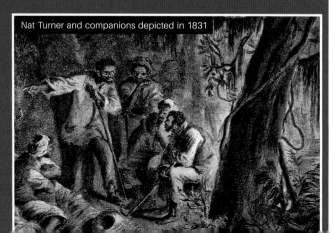

Nat Turner and companions depicted in 1831

On 24 February 2007, Virginia became the first state to acknowledge and publicly apologise for its history of slavery

"White American society remained aggressively opposed to equal rights"

Slaves on the plantation of the Confederate General Thomas F. Drayton, South Carolina 1862

THE INCREDIBLE HARRIET TUBMAN

Harriet Tubman was born into slavery in 1822 in Maryland. She was violently mistreated throughout her young life – at one point sustaining a serious head wound from a thrown metal weight, the after-effects of which remained with her for the rest of her life. But that life was a long and eventful one.

Aged 27, she escaped the plantation she was indentured on, making use of the 'Underground Railroad', a network of safe houses and abolitionist activists dedicated to helping slaves gain their freedom. She subsequently became prolifically active in the Railroad herself, undertaking daring missions back into Maryland to help rescue other slaves. She was so successful at it that the abolitionist William Lloyd Garrison dubbed her 'Moses'.

Tubman was a devout Christian who absolutely abhorred violence, but nevertheless later became a 'General' in John Brown's (ultimately unsuccessful) insurrectionist movement. When the Civil War broke out in 1861, she identified the Unionist cause as the one most likely to bring about an end to slavery, and worked as a scout and a spy in Confederate territory, helping to free slaves in their hundreds.

Well into her seventies, she became active in the fight for women's suffrage. She died from pneumonia, aged 91, in 1913, in a rest home named in her honour.

Harriet Tubman, photographed in 1900

PUBLIC

OF SL

FRANKLIN O

JAMES HARLAN'S Administrators, Plaintiffs,

vs.

JAMES HARLAN'S Heirs, Defendants,

The undersigned, as COMMI

Monday, Nov

(County Court day,) sell at public aucti

THREE NI

ONE NEGRO WOMAN AND

ONE NEGRO WOMAN

TERMS—Six months credit, with inte

with security, to have the force and eff

G

OCTOBER 30, 1863.

SALE
AVES!!

CUIT COURT.

Equity.

ONER of said Court, will, on

mber 16, 1863,

the following Slaves, viz:

GRO MEN;

SMALL CHILD, ADOPTED;

D TWO CHILDREN.

from date, the purchasers giving bond
f replevin bond.

RGE W. GWIN,
Master Commissioner.

KKK:
THE INVISIBLE ARMY

The Ku Klux Klan emerged in the aftermath of the American
Civil War and, in a number of iterations, practised horrific
violence and intimidation for more than 100 years

While identifying the origins of the Ku Klux Klan is straightforward, the motivations of those who joined this group are a little more complex, muddling racial and political purpose. Often cited as one of America's first terrorist organisations, the Klan was born in the South in the wake of the Confederacy's defeat in the Civil War, emerging when six former officers communed in Pulaski, Tennessee during May 1866 and organised what one of its founders described rather benignly as just "a club or society".

They took the name Ku Klux from the Greek word Kuklos, which means 'circle' or 'band', and granted themselves grandiose titles — such as Grand Cyclops, Grand Magi and Grand Turk — as they looked to imbue the society with an element of arcane mysticism. The group's founding came in the wake of a race riot in nearby Memphis, when a white mob clashed with a group of black Union soldiers, and the altercations sparked days of racial violence, resulting in the deaths of 46 black people and two white people.

The Ku Kluxers adopted intimidating outfits, robes and hoods, designed to hide their faces and to boost their height, and they galloped across the countryside, often claiming to be the ghosts of Confederate soldiers who had died in the war. With many of the freedmen still harbouring age-old superstitions, the Klan came to recognise that this proved an effective weapon against their primary targets, the freedmen and women. Indeed, it was this realisation to which one of the Klan founders, John Lester, attributed the transformation of the social club into a gang who set out to control the behaviour of the former slaves.

Most modern historians refute Lester's claim that the Klan was at its outset intended as nothing more than a social club, highlighting the fact that all six of its progenitors were raised in the South, fought for the Confederacy, and would therefore have practised an ingrained racism. Whatever the truth, there is no doubt that as the Klan grew in size and influence, it embraced ever more violent activity.

Its expansion was prompted in part by an intensifying political situation during 1866, as the Southerners railed against the Reconstruction policy imposed upon their states by politicians in the North. When the Republican Party voted to extend the power and influence of the Freedman's Bureau (designed to protect the rights of the former slaves), so the Klan numbers bloomed, with dens popping up all across the South. A presidential election loomed and the Klan began harassing black voters, urging them to vote for the Democrats, or even discouraging them from voting at all.

The Republican nominee, and former Union general, Ulysses S Grant, won the election in 1868 and in a scathing attack he claimed that the Klan's objectives were "by force and terror... to reduce the colored [sic] people to a condition closely allied to that of slavery". His reckoning drew on Klan members' political motives, though it should be noted that the Klan's intentions were only political in that the two American parties were split on racial issues.

For Klan members were first and foremost white supremacists. Sure, they said there should be equal rights for all men, but only those who were white. The black man, so many Southerners believed, was put upon this earth by God to serve white masters. The Klan attacked whites as well, targeting those whose attitude towards blacks differed from their own, most notably Southerners who had opposed secession and who supported black voting rights – so called 'scalawags' – and Northern whites who travelled to the South after the war to profit from Reconstruction. These were dubbed 'carpetbaggers'.

Klan action became increasingly violent during 1868, ranging from whippings of black women who were deemed insolent, or who had spurned white men's sexual advances, to the murder of white Republican leaders. When counting the numbers of attacks, the waters are muddied by historians' inability to disentangle local vigilante violence from the political terrorism dictated by the Klan. What is clear, however, is that attacks on black citizens became increasingly frequent. During the first ten-and-a-half months of 1868, the Freedman's Bureau reported 336 cases of murder or assault with intent to kill on freedmen in Georgia alone.

As the years ticked by, the violence continued, with Ku Kluxers regularly burning churches and schools that catered for freedmen, while they also sought to drive former slaves off the farms that they rented - a move that wrought much damage on the Southern economy. If any black, scalawag or carpetbagger sought recourse from the law they were unlikely to find it, with

"As the Klan grew, it embraced ever more violent activity"

many local law officers and magistrates in the South active Klan members.

Reports were made, however, and many Northerners bore witness to atrocity, provoking President Grant into action. In April 1871 he signed the Civil Rights Act, often called the Ku Klux Klan Act, a law that made it a federal offence to hinder a man's right to vote, hold office, serve on a jury or enjoy equal protection of the law.

Crucially, the Act also made it illegal for groups to conspire together or to wear disguises in order to harm people or to interfere with authorities seeking to protect citizens. As a federal law, anyone accused would be tried in federal, rather that state, courts. Grant and the federal government now had the tools to move against the KKK and, after a number of trials, were able to break it up.

Whether this was a great victory remains in dispute, and certainly in the following years many Americans rationalised and even romanticised the Klan's deeds, most notably in the popular novels, The Leopard's Spots (1902) and The Clansman (1905), as well as in the film The Birth Of A Nation (1915).

It came as no surprise, then, that a second iteration of the KKK emerged early in the 20th century, prompted in part by the success of The Birth Of A Nation and also by the notorious case of Leo Frank, a Jewish businessman

It is estimated that by the mid-1920s there might have been up to 5 million KKK members in the US

An induction ceremony for a new member of the Ku Klux Klan from the early 20th century

It's claimed that 50,000 KKK members marched on Washington in 1925, but other sources suggest it's closer to 200,000

"The black man, so many Southerners believed, was put upon this earth by God to serve white masters"

THE BIRTH OF A NATION

Directed by celebrated filmmaker D.W. Griffith and adapted from the novel and play *The Clansman* by Thomas Dixon Jr, *The Birth Of A Nation* is one of early Hollywood's most famous, and infamous, silent-era epics. The film chronicles the relationship of two families in the American Civil War and Reconstruction era, and though a huge commercial success, it attracted controversy for its portrayal of black men (many played by white actors) as brutish, lazy, morally degenerate, and dangerous. Its romantic presentation of the Ku Klux Klan, meanwhile, is widely credited with inspiring the founding of the Klan's second iteration, which rose in 1916, the year after the film's national release.

For all the controversy of its subject matter, *The Birth Of A Nation* is recognised as an important piece of technical filmmaking - it's seen by many film historians as the first piece of cinematic realism - and in 1992 the United States Library of Congress deemed the film "culturally, historically, or aesthetically significant" and selected it for preservation in the National Film Registry. According to one prominent film historian and critic, "The worst thing about *The Birth Of A Nation* is how good it is."

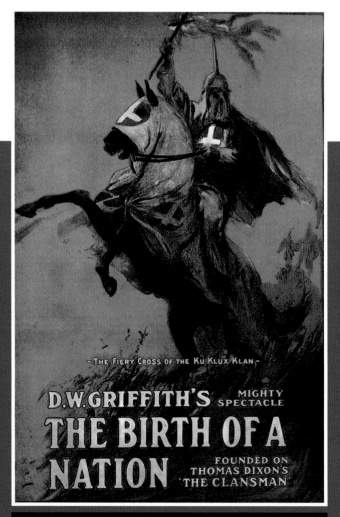

D.W. Griffith's self-proclaimed "mighty spectacle" did much to usher in a new era of KKK activity following its release in 1915

Ku Klux Klan annual congress, York, Pennsylvania, September 1937

LYNCHING: AN AMERICAN DISEASE

Lynching, or the public murder by a mob of an individual suspected of a crime, appears to be a peculiarly American problem. While lynching certainly pre-dates the Civil War, in its aftermath public hangings and shootings became something of an epidemic in the South, especially with the rise of the KKK. Hanging and shooting were the primary methods of lynching, though the sadism of its practitioners also saw burning at the stake, maiming, dismemberment, castration, and other brutal methods.

There are no reliable statistics for the number of lynchings prior to 1882 and those compiled after that date are by no means complete. That said, according to figures from the Tuskegee Institute between the years 1882-1951, 4,730 people were lynched in the US, of which 3,437 were black and 1,293 were white. The Institute claims that the largest number of lynchings occurred in 1892, when 230 people were killed — 161 black, and 69 white.

During the 1920s the number of lynchings began to tail off as the South became ever more urbanised and attitudes began to soften. The passing of the 1922 Dyer Anti-Lynching Bill in the House of Representatives also proved important, announcing fines and imprisonment for anyone convicted of lynching, to be enforced by federal rather than state courts.

In addition, it announced fines and penalties against states, counties, and towns that failed to protect citizens from mob violence. The Senate blocked the bill, Southern politicians claiming that anti-lynching legislation was unconstitutional, though the discussions and attention that the bill provoked proved to be of great importance.

"Crucially, the Act also made it illegal for groups to conspire together or to wear disguises in order to harm people"

who was convicted of raping and murdering a 13-year-old girl. It owes its inception to William J. Simmons, who along with 16 others, ascended Stone Mountain (about 16 kilometres northeast of downtown Atlanta, Georgia) and, under the light of a burning cross, announced the rebirth of the Knights of the Ku Klux Klan.

Membership of the second Klan grew slowly during World War I, but exploded across the South in the 1920s thanks in no small part to the influence of the Southern Publicity Association who proved masters at PR, reaching out to more moderate white Americans, tapping into fears they harboured in the wake of the Great War. They declaimed not only black people, Catholics and Jews, but also Bolsheviks, putting the order forward as the militant defender of "pure Americanism", "old-time religion" and upstanding morality. It is estimated that it once boasted as many as five million members.

Given its size, the Klan gained wide political influence in the 1920s, with the state governments of Alabama, Colorado, Georgia, Indiana, Louisiana, Oklahoma, Oregon, and Texas featuring a number of Klan members among their officials. Emboldened and encouraged, the Klan once more visited terrible atrocity on those it deemed unworthy. Such was the escalation of lynching in Georgia, for example, by October 1923 African Americans were leaving the state for the North at a rate of 1,500 per month.

It was at the very height of its political influence that the second Klan began to decline and fall, undermined by internal feuding, increased activism by opponents, and the fading of its romantic image. By 1930 Klan numbers fell to around 30,000.

Again, though, it refused to die, and emerged once more after World War II, offering extremely violent resistance to the Civil Rights Movement as it fought the federal mandates for desegregation.

Messrs Redmond, Roberson and Addison, accused of the murder of Marshal Carter of Toccoa, were taken from jail by a mob and lynched in May 1892

The Ku Klux Klan offered extremely violent resistance to attempts to try to desegregate the South. This cross burning from 1956 is notable due to the number of young people involved.

FROM
EMANCIPATION
TO EXPECTATION

Progressing from freedom to self-sufficiency, the black experience following the Civil War and into the 20th Century was fraught with challenge and opposition

A fter President Abraham Lincoln issued the Emancipation Proclamation on 1 January 1863, two more bloody years of civil war remained. Even after the Union victory, the uncertainty of the future for the newly freed black population of the South was an open question.

Slavery had been a stabilising factor in the economy of the South, and inherent in the transformation of former slaves to free people a prolonged period of instability followed. The years of Reconstruction were, in fact, the imposition of martial law and military occupation of the states of the former Confederacy with the exception of Tennessee. Federal troops were stationed in the Deep South to maintain order and protect black citizens from the retaliation of resentful whites, as well as to allow blacks to take advantage of opportunities for education, to work for themselves, exercise the rights to vote and hold office, and become self-sufficient.

While the 13th Amendment to the US Constitution, ratified on 6 December 1865, abolished slavery, the 14th Amendment, ratified on 9 July 1868, granted former slaves citizenship, and the 15th Amendment, ratified on 3 February 1870, granted black men the right to vote, ordinary citizens experienced the struggle for equality on a grass roots level. Legislation could make a statement, but practical application was slowed by systemic racism, violence at the hands of organisations such as the Ku Klux Klan, and local laws that allowed little change in the condition of freed slaves from the days of enslavement.

By 1870, a total of 22 black representatives had been elected to Congress. Freedmen, as former slaves were called, were becoming more literate. Wages were paid to freedmen who worked. Former abolitionists from the North, church groups, and concerned citizens helped freed slaves to learn to read and function more fully. These were pioneers in the cause of civil rights.

Still, the question of the status of free blacks persisted. The white power structure, though curbed somewhat, remained dominant despite the presence of federal soldiers, who eventually departed in 1877 amid mixed results in assimilating both black communities and white populations into a

An officer of a government agency known as the Freedmen's Bureau holds off a crowd of angry white citizens

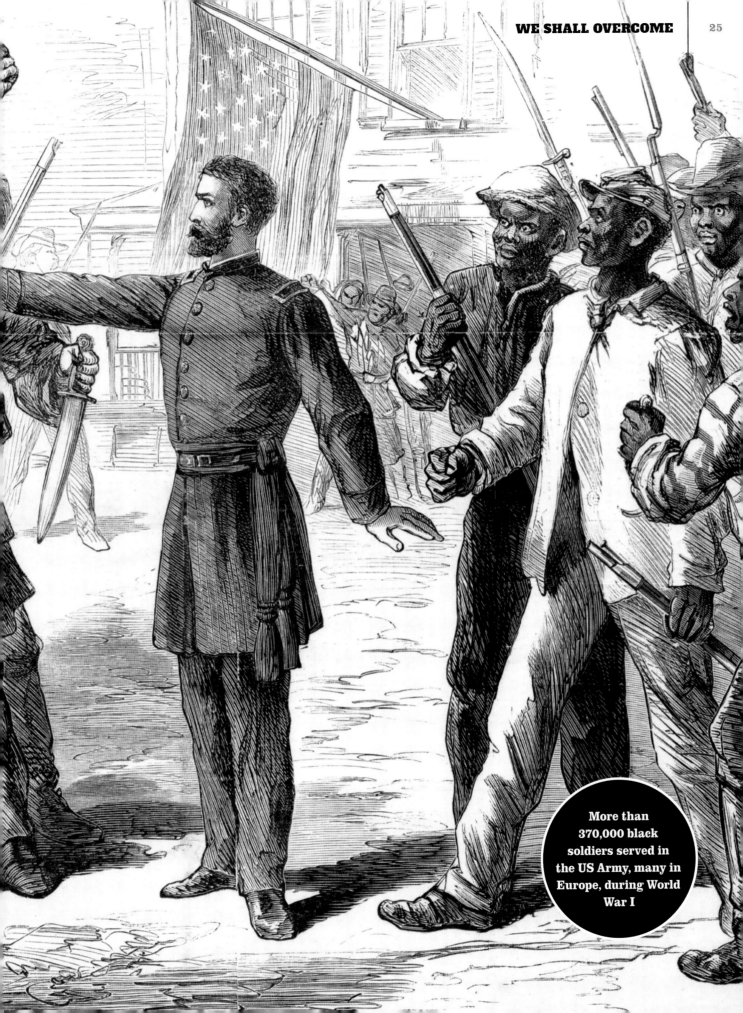

More than 370,000 black soldiers served in the US Army, many in Europe, during World War I

functioning society.

In the wake of the Civil War, Southern state governments feared the implications of racial equality, and as early as 1865 enacted laws known as the 'Black Codes' to prevent former slaves from improving their economic and social status. The codes reinforced a condition of white supremacy, and decades of struggle, protest, violence, triumph, and tragedy followed as the civil rights movement found its footing in the mid-20th century.

Beginning in the late 1800s, Southern legislatures began passing a series of laws collectively referred to by the derisive term 'Jim Crow' after a stereotypical black theatre character popularised during the 1830s. These laws affirmed segregation in the South, while other states across America enacted measures that might be considered racist in their own right and classified as Jim Crow. Among the most blatant Jim Crow discrimination were measures against interracial marriage, mandates for separate schools, and separate public facilities, such as theatres and restaurants. Laws regarding transportation restricted black people to certain sections on trains, and later they were required to take seats at the back of public buses.

In 1896, the US Supreme Court voted 7 to 1 to uphold the doctrine of "separate but equal" with the landmark Plessy v Ferguson decision. The court ruled that racial segregation laws regarding public facilities were constitutional as long as those facilities were comparable. For the next half a century, the court considered measures that diminished the overreach of Plessy v Ferguson but never fully repudiated the decision. Among these cases, Brown v the Board of Education of Topeka, Kansas, required the desegregation of the district's public schools in 1954, nearly 60 years after Plessy v Ferguson.

Waves of voter suppression, racist legislation, vigilante justice, and outright violence persisted during the early years of so-called freedom for

"Decades of struggle, protest, violence, triumph, and tragedy followed as the movement found its footing"

Northern teachers moved to the South to assist former slaves in becoming literate during Reconstruction

Four-time gold medallist Jesse Owens begins a record-breaking sprint to victory during the 200 metres at the 1936 Olympics

THE ELECTRIFYING JESSE OWENS

At the height of the power and influence of the Nazi Party in Germany, its capital city, Berlin, hosted the 1936 Summer Olympics. Although stories of Nazi persecution of Jews and other minorities in the Third Reich had surfaced, the Germans worked to present a façade of friendship in welcoming the world's athletes. Adolf Hitler and his Nazi regime remained confident in the superiority of their 'Master Race' and expected such to be proven during the athletic competition.

Among the members of the American Olympic team was a black 22-year-old track and field star named Jesse Owens, who had already achieved notoriety with his accomplishments in domestic competition. Now on the world stage, Owens singlehandedly shattered the myth of Nazi Aryan racial supremacy, winning four gold medals. Owens dazzled the crowd with victories in the 100 metres, 200 metres, long jump, and 4x100 metre relay. The spectators roared as Hitler looked on in disbelief.

Still, Owens remembered, "When I came back to my native country, after all the stories about Hitler, I couldn't ride in the front of the bus... I wasn't invited to shake hands with Hitler, but I wasn't invited to the White House to shake hands with the President, either."

blacks in the South. From 1884 to 1900, more than 2,000 black people were lynched, often without interference from law enforcement. Most of these victims were accused of trumped-up crimes ranging from fraternisation with white women to rape or murder. Sometimes without formal charges or trials, they were dragged to trees and summarily hanged with great spectacle as angry crowds gathered to witness the grisly scenes.

The era that preceded the awakening of the Civil Rights Movement in the 1950s spanned nearly a century, and being black in the United States meant living in a period of overt discrimination, limited access to education, jobs, and even healthcare. In 1900, the average life expectancy of a black man in America was 33 years. For a white man it was 47.6 years. By 1978, the gap had closed to 69.2 years versus 74 years. The implication is clear – black people were consigned to the lower rung of the socio-economic ladder, often victims

W.E.B. Du Bois was a co-founder of the NAACP, prominent sociologist, and civil rights activist

Booker T. Washington speaks to a rapt audience including Mark Twain (behind the speaker) at Carnegie Hall in New York City

Among the most significant political voices of the period was Booker T. Washington, a member of the black generation born into slavery and then experiencing the social evolution of the times. Washington was an author, educator, and advisor to US presidents. He advocated black education and entrepreneurship in response to Jim Crow, and his platform was a historically black college, Tuskegee Institute, in Alabama. Other outspoken black reformers chose a more aggressive line. A leader of this faction was W.E.B. Du Bois, the first black person to earn a doctorate degree from Harvard University. Du Bois believed that the black intellectual elite should lead the fight for equal rights and refused to acquiesce to the terms of the Atlanta Convention advocated by Washington. Du Bois was a co-founder of the National Association for the Advancement of Colored People (NAACP) in 1909, a strong voice for civil rights to this day.

In 1903, Du Bois prophetically proclaimed that the single greatest issue of the 20th century was the "color line". During the years preceding World War II, his statement was proven in the persistence of segregation and discrimination not only in the South, but also across the United States. Traditionally, the Republican Party had provided support for black people, but during the 1930s the role of the Democratic Party, previously the oppressor, began to change. In 1934, Arthur W Mitchell became the first black man elected to Congress as a Democrat. In sports, Branch Rickey, owner of the Brooklyn Dodgers, committed to signing Jackie Robinson, who broke major league baseball's colour barrier, to a contract in 1945.

By then, the experience of World War II was changing the character of American society. The Holocaust revealed the depths of depravity that racism could plumb. The Great Migration had contributed to black social mobility, and the political arena had changed. These forces converged as catalysts for the Civil Rights Movement that would grow during the 1950s from the realisation that there was still much work to be done.

of a cycle of poverty and disadvantage that precluded upward mobility, a fundamental component of the American dream.

Despite these difficulties, African Americans made inroads, not only achieving notable successes in the South, but also migrating in large numbers to Northern and Midwestern cities, where their industriousness paid dividends and a cultural renaissance flourished. In the midst of this so-called Great Migration, black entertainers were often relegated to stereotypical roles, particularly in the burgeoning film industry; however, their achievements in literature, theatre, music and athletics succeeded in blurring – if not completely erasing – the colour barrier.

MARCUS GARVEY AND PAN-AFRICANISM

Jamaican-born Marcus Garvey rose to become a champion of Pan-Africanism, advocating solidarity among all people of African descent. In 1914, he founded the Universal Negro Improvement Association and African Communities League (UNIA-ACL). Garvey was an outspoken proponent of African people returning to their native continent and actually started a shipping company, the Black Star Line, to facilitate the movement of black people and commercial goods produced by blacks around the world.

Garvey's policies were controversial, including the fact that he favoured racial segregation, and he drew significant criticism from other black leaders. Despite this, he also gained a large following. His activities further attracted the attention of the US government, and the Bureau of Investigation, forerunner of the FBI, placed him under surveillance. In the early 1920s, the Black Star Line foundered. Garvey was arrested for mail fraud related to his selling stock in the company. He was sentenced to prison and deported to Jamaica in 1927.

Months later, Garvey founded Jamaica's first political party. In 1935, he emigrated to Britain and monitored the tragic war that was unfolding as fascist Italy attacked the East African nation of Ethiopia. He died of a stroke in 1940 at the age of 52.

Marcus Garvey, a leader in the Pan-Africanism movement, poses in 1924, after the failure of the Black Star Line

THE FOUNDING FATHERS OF CIVIL RIGHTS

Though their views frequently clashed, W.E.B. Du Bois and Marcus Garvey laid the foundations of the modern Civil Rights Movement

William Edward Burghardt Du Bois aged 50, in 1918

The campaigns for civil rights that began in 1954 and led to the legislative victories of the 1960s produced two images of leadership. Martin Luther King Jr. advocated the assertion of equal rights in law, voting and education for black Americans. Malcolm X saw the struggle for black American rights as a global one, and advocated separatism, the creation of a separate black economy and sovereignty. Both of these strategies had roots in 19th and early 20th century history, in the rivalry between William Edward Burghardt (W E B) Du Bois and Marcus Garvey.

The Northern states won the Civil War, but the end of slavery did not lead to the end of discrimination. In the Southern states, 'Jim Crow' laws segregated blacks from whites. In the Northern states, including the cities to which Southern blacks migrated in search of jobs and equality, discrimination continued through informal racism.

W.E.B. Du Bois was born in 1868 to a family who had been 'free blacks' during the era of slavery. He grew up in the farming town of Great Barrington, Massachusetts, and attended a racially mixed school. When he left, he was granted the honour of delivering the 'valedictorian', or farewell speech, on behalf of his entire grade. Du Bois then moved south, to attend the all-black Fisk University in Tennessee. There, he began to see the extent of the Jim Crow laws, and the open racism and violence that accompanied them. The experience shocked him, and he returned to Massachusetts to devote himself to the struggle for equal rights.

In 1895, Du Bois became the first black man to obtain a PhD from Harvard. His dissertation, on 'The Suppression of the African Slave Trade to the United States of America, 1638-1870', was one of the first works on the subject. By the turn of the century, Du Bois had returned to the South, as a professor at Atlanta University in Georgia. He had established himself as a rising black intellectual, which brought him into conflict with another eminent American black thinker of the time, Booker T. Washington.

Washington had been born a slave in the mid 1850s, and worked in a salt

> **Du Bois' reporting helped bring national attention to the East St. Louis riots, where dozens of black Americans were massacred**

mine and as a domestic servant before obtaining an education at the Hampton Institute, one of the first all-black schools in the United States. As the leader of the Tuskegee Institute in Alabama, an all-black vocational school, Washington had practised his belief that Southern blacks, like Southern whites, needed agricultural and technical training if they were to survive in the industrial economy. Washington believed that, if Southern blacks could obtain economic independence and demonstrate their practical value to their Southern white neighbours, then the Southern whites would grant them civil equality.

Washington's strategy became known as the 'Atlanta Compromise', after the Georgia capital where Washington had announced it in 1895. Washington's numerous white supporters, among them many Southern politicians and President Theodore Roosevelt, praised this strategy as restrained and patriotic. His critics, Du Bois included, claimed that this policy was a permanent compromise, and an accommodation to an unacceptable system. Washington, they said, deferred the difficult and necessary political campaign for civil rights to an unspecified future.

The 1899 lynching of Sam Hose in Georgia by a mob of up to 2,000 whites reconfirmed Du Bois' conviction that urgent action, not sentiment, was required. Hose was tortured, hanged, and then burned. Du Bois, walking to a meeting with a sympathetic newspaper editor, saw Hose's scorched knuckles on display in an Atlanta shop window. In 1903, Du Bois published the essay collection The Souls of Black Folk, a watershed in African American literature, and an open repudiation of Washington's accommodationist strategy.

"The Problem of the 20th century is the color line," Du Bois wrote, "the relation of the darker to the lighter races of men in Asia and Africa, in America and the islands of the sea." All blacks, but especially Southern blacks, needed both legal equality and the social equality that came from education. Washington's Atlanta Compromise was a strategy for 'conciliation'. It would continue 'the old attitude of adjustment and submission', and regardless of whether it persuaded Southern whites to grant legal equality, it would create a new subjection, this time purely economic.

Drawing on his experience at Harvard and Atlanta, Du Bois advocated the training of a black elite, a 'Talented Tenth' who could pursue "the loftiest of ideals" and strive for "culture and character", rather than economic subsistence. In the Southern states, he said, blacks and whites were segregated, and the police and the judicial system functioned as "a means of re-enslaving the blacks". If blacks were to obtain equality in law and opportunity, they must cultivate their own educational, political and spiritual resources. In 1905, Du Bois and several other young African American campaigners

> *"Hose was tortured, hanged, and then burned. Du Bois [later] saw Hose's scorched knuckles on display in an Atlanta shop window"*

Marcus Garvey in his trademark tricorn hat, 1922

FORGOTTEN EARLY CIVIL RIGHTS HEROES

Edward Wilmot Blyden
Born in the Danish West Indies (now the US Virgin Islands), Edward Blyden was a teacher, politician and 'the father of pan-Africanism'. In 1850, after American colleges had refused his application to study as a minister, he moved to Liberia, where he served as secretary of state.

Prince Hall
Prince Hall claimed to have been born of African parentage in England in the mid-1730s. Brought to Boston as either a servant or a slave, he trained as a tanner, and eventually secured his freedom. In 1773, he was part of a free black group that petitioned the Massachusetts Senate for their return to Africa. Soon afterwards, however, he rallied blacks in support of the American Revolution.

Martin Delany
Martin Delany (1812-1885) was born to an enslaved father and a free mother, and grew up with his mother's free status. In Pittsburgh, he became an advocate for creating a 'Black Israel' in East Africa, a campaigner for abolition, and a founding theorist of black nationalism. Accepted to Harvard Medical School and then expelled after white students protested, he became the only black major in the Union army.

Booker T. Washington
Booker T. Washington (1856-1915) came from the last generation of black leaders to be born into slavery. In the 1890s, he became the dominant voice in the American black community. Though his 'Atlanta Compromise' was discredited by W.E.B. Du Bois, Washington was an inspiration to both Du Bois and Marcus Garvey.

Fredrick McGhee
Born a slave in Mississippi, Fredrick McGhee (1861-1912) became one of America's first black lawyers, and laid the cornerstones of the modern Civil Rights Movement. In 1905, he joined W.E.B. Du Bois in founding the Niagara Movement, whose campaign for civil rights led in turn to the founding of the NAACP in 1909.

founded Niagara, a movement whose principles explicitly rejected the Atlanta Compromise.

Events vindicated Du Bois' criticism of Washington's approach. In 1906, President Roosevelt dishonourably discharged 167 black soldiers in response to the Brownsville Affair, in which the white residents of Brownsville, Texas had rioted against the presence of black soldiers. Soon afterwards, more than 200 blacks were murdered by white mobs at Atlanta. The Compromise, Du Bois wrote, in 'A Litany at Atlanta', was over.

The consensus among black activists now swung towards campaigning for equal rights, free votes and educational opportunity. In 1910, Du Bois moved to New York and began working as the Director of Publicity and Research for the organisation that would lead the next phase of the campaign, the National Association for the Advancement of Colored People (NAACP). In this office, he led campaigns against lynchings, the segregation of the US Army, and D.W. Griffith's 1915 film The Birth Of A Nation, which portrayed the Ku Klux Klan as patriotic defenders of American values.

Du Bois had always seen the 'colour line' as a global problem. In The Souls of Black Folk, he had analysed the "double consciousness" of American blacks as a harmful psychological split between black and American identities. Healing this division required not just equality in American law and society, but also the strengthening of links with other non-white populations – and, in Du Bois' estimation, the embracing of anti-imperial and socialist politics. As early as 1900, he had attended the first Pan-African conference, organised in London by Haitian and Trinidadian campaigners. In 1919, while in Paris gathering information on discrimination in the US Army, Du Bois attended the first of a series of Pan-African Conferences.

In the early years of the century, Du Bois had outflanked the older Booker T. Washington, by advocating immediate legal equality rather than economic integration and accommodation to the existing order. Now, Du Bois found himself accused of being an accommodationist. His new, and younger, antagonist was Marcus Garvey (1887-1940), the Jamaican-born proponent of black separatism and going 'Back to Africa'.

Ironically, Booker T. Washington's vision of black economic independence was one of the inspirations of the Universal Negro Improvement Association (UNIA), which Garvey founded in 1914. Two years later, Garvey was in America, soliciting funds for a Jamaican technical institute in the style of Washington's own Tuskegee Institute. Yet Garvey shared none of Washington's accommodationist politics. Nor, though he shared Du Bois' conviction that the problems of black Americans were also global ones, did he share Du Bois' hopes that the equalities of law and socialism would cure racist attitudes among whites.

By 1920, the UNIA claimed to have four million members. Garvey had survived an assassination attempt, and launched a program to modernise the infrastructure of Liberia, the West African state established by ex-American slaves, and which Garvey wanted to turn into a model black state. He had also created the Black Star Line, a shipping line intended to help build up economic links between Africa and the rest of the world, and to export skilled and committed American blacks to Liberia.

Du Bois, whose NAACP magazine The Crisis was the biggest black publication in America, praised the spirit of the Black Star Line, but called Garvey "the most dangerous enemy of the Negro race in America and the

The Niagara Movement, 1905. Du Bois, in the middle row, wears a white hat

The Yarmouth, the first ship in the Black Star Line's short-lived fleet

Group portrait of the delegates to the Niagara Movement meeting in Boston, Massachusetts in 1907

The Silent Parade, New York, 1917, organised by Du Bois to protest race riots in St. Louis

world". The FBI agreed, and prosecuted Garvey for using an image of a ship not owned by the Black Star Line on a brochure soliciting funds for it. In 1922, Garvey was sentenced to five years in prison, and the Black Star Line went under. In 1927, President Coolidge ordered his deportation to Jamaica. He would eventually die in London, in 1940.

Meanwhile, Du Bois rose to ever-greater eminence. He enthused about the flourishing of the arts among the growing black population in New York City – the 'Harlem Renaissance' – and moved between the university and left-wing politics. While his strategies for civil rights in America became the mainstream ideas of the 1960s movement, his international perspective and his political views remained subjects of controversy. He died in Ghana in 1963, aged 95.

Du Bois was more socialist and pan-African in his politics than Martin Luther King Jr. and less Christian too. Malcolm X shared much of Garvey's separatism and back-to-Africa philosophy. But regardless, King and Malcolm X, the universalist and the particularist, marched in the lineage of Du Bois and Garvey.

THE SOUTH UNDER JIM CROW

Segregation in the Southern States of America was legally entrenched in laws unofficially named after a popular racist song

"**W**heel about and turn about and do just so, every time I wheel about I jump Jim Crow..." So ran the chorus to the Jump Jim Crow song: 44 verses of racist doggerel made popular by the white 19th century performer Thomas 'Daddy' Rice. Rice performed the popular number dressed in rags, a battered hat and worn-out shoes, with his face, of course, blackened. The lyrics covered the mischief he got up to, often at the expense of white people. The piece was a forerunner of the minstrel shows that helped spread the stereotype of the lazy, uneducated and violent black man far and wide. It also gave its name to the laws that kept black people segregated from whites for decades.

The so-called Jim Crow laws evolved from the Black Codes passed in the Southern states of America in the 1860s. These in turn came out of the pre-Civil War Slave Codes defining the status of slaves and the responsibilities of slave owners. The Black Codes applied to the former slaves recently emancipated by the events of 1861-1865. Their purpose was to control the movement and labour of black people, and to keep them politically and socially suppressed. They may have been free, but to white folk of the South, they would never be equal.

By the 1870s the period of Reconstruction had seen legislation introduced to protect the civil rights of African Americans. These small positive steps were, however, almost immediately reversed by the white politicians, who quickly regained political power in almost all of the Southern states. Those black candidates who had managed to achieve political voice found their votes suppressed in state and national elections, and without representation, the black inhabitants of the Southern states were officially disenfranchised.

The white supremacists stamped down hard on the very idea of the creation of a black middle class. Segregation meant separate schools and public facilities (even down to separate drinking fountains) for black people, and those facilities were grossly underfunded and unsupported.

African Americans in the South were condemned to lives of poverty and illiteracy, their societal suppression and abuse officially sanctioned. Barely even viewed as citizens, and certainly as sub-class, black people could not even rely on the justice system when crimes were perpetrated against them. Lynchings remained commonplace in the South throughout the first half of the 20th century, taking place in the thousands. It wasn't until the shocking murder of Emmett Till gained widespread press attention in 1955 that attitudes finally began to shift.

Specific laws varied from state to state, but everywhere in the Jim Crow South you could expect to be allocated a seat on public transport according to your colour. White nurses were not required to work on hospital wards upon which black patients had been placed. Black hairdressers and barbers were forbidden from cutting Caucasian hair. Intermarriage and cohabiting were completely illegal. In Mississippi, printing, publishing and circulating any material suggesting that black and white people were equal was punishable with a $500 fine or six months in prison. In Louisiana, public shows like circuses and outdoor events were required by law to operate two separate ticket offices – one for white spectators, and another for black. In Georgia it was unlawful for black and white amateur baseball teams to play within two blocks of one another.

More than 360,000 black American soldiers fought in World War I, but they returned only to race riots: black soldiers in uniform were lynched by white mobs. The National Association for the Advancement of Colored People (the NAACP) was formed to draw attention to the injustices that black Americans were suffering daily. But it wasn't until WWII that the tide finally began to turn. The resemblance of the Third Reich's desire for a master race with that of the white supremacist South to remain racially pure became politically embarrassing for the US on the world stage. President Harry Truman urged Congress to begin dismantling the Jim Crow laws in 1948. Integrated troops fought together for the first time in the Korean War.

There was still a long way to go, but civil rights activists began to enjoy more victories as their cause gained political and social momentum over the coming years.

"Printing, publishing and circulating any material suggesting that black and white people were equal was punishable"

The Supreme Court upheld segregationist rulings at least six more times in the 60 years following Plessy v Ferguson

The Jim Crow stereotype as popularised by Thomas Rice

Campaigners protest against military segregation in 1948

Segregated school following Plessy v Ferguson in 1896

Symbolic funeral for Jim Crow in a 1944 demonstration

PLESSY V FERGUSON, 1896

While "separate but equal" might seem like a ridiculous description of the divide between black and white people in the American South under the Jim Crow laws, it was nevertheless language inscribed in law. The landmark Supreme Court ruling for Plessy v Ferguson, upholding segregation as constitutional, was issued in 1896.

Homer Plessy was officially deemed to be black, even though he was seven-eighths of European heritage and only one-eighth African. To test this judgement of his lineage, on 7 June 1892, he bought a first-class ticket for the whites-only car of a New Orleans train and duly took his seat. When he refused to move to the blacks-only car at the back of the train, he was arrested. At the trial, presiding Judge John Howard Ferguson upheld the right of the State of Louisiana to segregate as it saw fit, and fined Plessy $25. Plessy and the Citizens Committee of New Orleans appealed, but the Supreme Court upheld Ferguson's ruling.

The case legitimised the South's segregationist laws and policies, and laid the ground for the so-called Jim Crow laws of the 20th century. Despite its de facto overturning by the Brown v Board of Education case in 1954, Plessy v Ferguson has never actually been officially repealed.

A CHANGE IS GONNA COME

17 May 1954

BROWN V THE BOARD OF EDUCATION

By 1954 – and almost the entirety of the 20th century up until that point – American children had attended racially segregated schools. Since 1896, the contradictory policy of 'separate but equal' was enforced, forcing students to ride separate school buses, attend different schools and grow up as divided as adult society. The NAACP (National Association for the Advancement of Colored People) had fought for decades in courts across the nation to amend the law, and it would be one such case that would eventually overturn half a century of segregation for good.

That case was filed by 13 parents from Topeka, Kansas, led by welder and assistant pastor Oliver Brown. It claimed that the facilities provided by the state for African American students were far from equal to those of their white pupils and were, as a result, unconstitutional. Brown's own daughter had been barred from all of Topeka's all-white elementary schools, forcing her to travel much further afield to one deemed suitable for people of colour. Claiming this was an affront to the 14th Amendment rights of every African American, the US District Court in Kansas agreed that such division had caused a "detrimental effect upon the colored children," but upheld the "separate but equal" doctrine.

So Brown and his fellow plaintiffs combined their cause with a number of other similar cases and appealed to the Supreme Court in 1952 under Brown v the Board of Education of Topeka. With Thurgood Marshall, the head of the NAACP Legal Defense and Educational Fund, acting as their chief attorney, the case would eventually lead to a landslide victory for Brown, with a unanimous decision stating that the segregation policy was both unethical and unconstitutional, and that by law all schools were to begin reintegrating races.

Despite the ruling, progress was slow. By 1964, only about 1% of black children in the South attended school with whites

Thurgood Marshall celebrates with attorneys George E.C. Hayes and James M. Nabrit outside the Supreme Court following the landmark ruling

• Founding Of The SCLC
10 January 1957

Formed by Martin Luther King Jr. in January 1957 following the Montgomery Bus Boycott, the Southern Christian Leadership Conference was created to further the movement through nonviolent means. By forming the crux of its membership through churches, the SCLC gained a massive following, and played a key role in civil rights for African Americans.

• The Greensboro sit-ins
1 February - 25 July 1960

Far from the only sit-in of its time, the protests in Greensboro, North Carolina, were the most famous and were instrumental in the wider movement. African American students Joseph McNeil, Franklin McCain, Ezell Blair Jr. and David Richmond took seats in the local Woolworth department store and refused to move for over five months. It led to the chain removing its segregation policy.

• Freedom Rider Movement
4 May - 10 December 1961

For seven months in 1961, a group of civil rights activists began riding on buses across the United States in reaction to the non-enforcement of two Supreme Court rulings that deemed segregation on public buses as unconstitutional. Over 430 activists conducted 60 Freedom Rides over this time, with the violent response from KKK members and even some police precincts only serving to bolster the Civil Rights Movement.

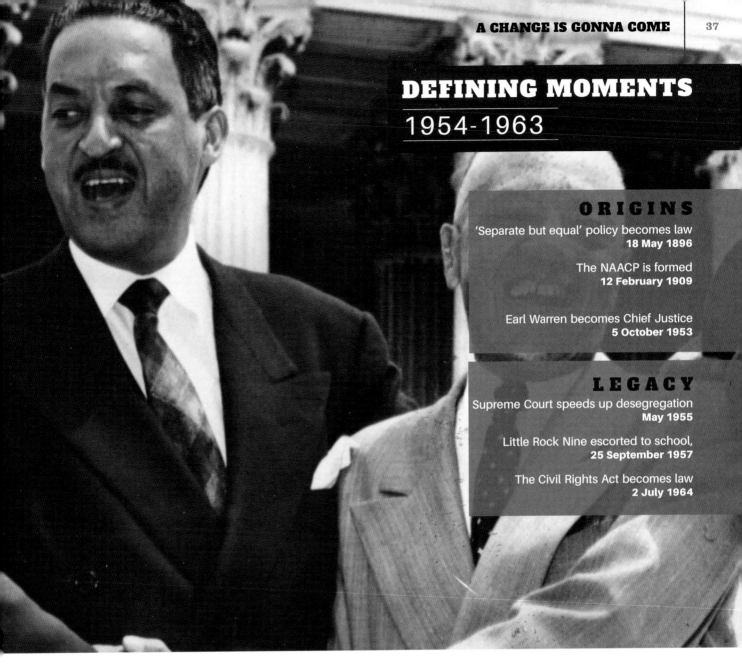

DEFINING MOMENTS
1954-1963

ORIGINS
'Separate but equal' policy becomes law
18 May 1896

The NAACP is formed
12 February 1909

Earl Warren becomes Chief Justice
5 October 1953

LEGACY
Supreme Court speeds up desegregation
May 1955

Little Rock Nine escorted to school,
25 September 1957

The Civil Rights Act becomes law
2 July 1964

The Integration Of Ole Miss
30 September – 1 October 1962

In September 1962, African American military veteran James Meredith applied to study at the University of Mississippi (known as 'Ole Miss'). Following the victory of the Brown v the Board of Education case in 1954, Meredith was within his rights to attend, but the case caused outrage and led to a two-day riot where over 300 were injured and two were left dead. Meredith graduated on 18 August 1963, with a degree in political science.

JFK's Civil Rights Address
11 June 1963

When president John F. Kennedy delivered what became known as the 'Report to the American People on Civil Rights' speech in 1963, his words transformed the Civil Rights Movement forever. JFK implored the nation to consider the fight for equality not as a legal issue, but a moral one, and stated publicly that he would be personally backing new legislation that would see these issues finally recognised.

The Assassination Of
Medgar Evers 12 June 1963

Mere hours after JFK's famous Civil Rights Address, prominent activist and NAACP field secretary Medgar Evers was fatally shot through the heart by Byron De La Beckwith, a member of the White Citizens' Council and the Ku Klux Klan. Evers, a World War II veteran, was buried with full honours, and his death ultimately proved another vital piece in the fight for African American civil rights.

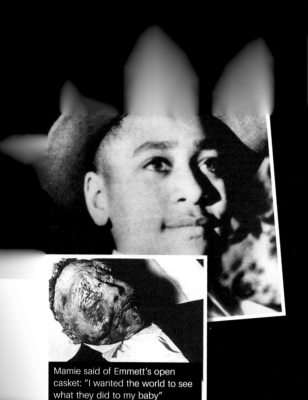

MURDER THAT SHOCKED AMERICA

The horrifying lynching of Emmett Till by two white racists was an important catalyst for the American Civil Rights Movement

Mamie said of Emmett's open casket: "I wanted the world to see what they did to my baby"

Emmett Till could have had no idea that he would still be remembered more than 60 years after his death, or that he would be seen as in any way significant to an important cause. Tragically, his death was more significant than his short life.

Till was born on 25 July 1941. Essentially raised by a single mother, Mamie (a violent father and stepfather made sporadic appearances), he grew up in Chicago, but was fascinated by the stories of the old days in the Mississippi Delta he heard from his great-uncle Mose. In the summer of 1955, aged just 14, he made the fateful decision to visit the segregated South where his mother was raised. Mamie warned him that it was a far more racially charged environment than Chicago, and that he must be very careful how he comported himself in white company. He promised he'd be careful.

Till initially settled in well in Money, Mississippi, the town where Mose was a local preacher. Till made friends quickly among the children of the local sharecroppers, but after only three days of his vacation, the events that would lead to the violent end of his young life began to spiral. While his friends played in the street, he went to buy two cents' worth of bubble gum from the grocery shop that was owned by a white couple called Roy and Carolyn Bryant.

Carolyn was working alone at the time, and would claim that Till grabbed her and made lascivious suggestions – a story she retracted later in life. Other witnesses stated that Till did almost nothing to attract attention to himself. He may have whistled at Carolyn as he left the store, but even there, contradictory reports have suggested that the whistle may have been a technique he used to combat his stutter, or that he was simply trying to attract the attention of a friend playing checkers across the street.

Whatever the truth, the idea of a black boy behaving in a familiar fashion towards a white woman was not one that could be tolerated in the racist South of the United States where lynchings were still relatively commonplace. When Roy Bryant learned of the altercation, he flew into a rage. Enlisting the help of his half-brother John William Milam, he began a search for Emmett Till, which three days later, led him to the home of Mose and his family. Bryant and Milam then forced entry, and dragged Till out of the house to a waiting pickup truck.

They drove him to a barn in Drew, Mississippi, pistol-whipped him, brutally beat him and eventually shot him in the head. They then weighted his body and threw it in the Tallahatchie River, where it surfaced on 31 August.

Unlike previous similar murders, however, Till's grisly and unjust end would not go unremarked. Early as Till's death was in the history of the Civil Rights Movement, the times he was living in were nevertheless politically and racially charged enough for the events in Money and Drew to make headline news across the United States. This had much to do with the fact that Till hailed from Chicago rather than the South, and with Mamie's decision to display Emmett's mutilated and unrecog-

Mamie with Emmett's great-uncle Mose

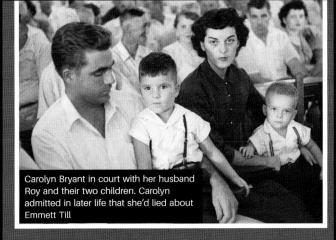

Carolyn Bryant in court with her husband Roy and their two children. Carolyn admitted in later life that she'd lied about Emmett Till

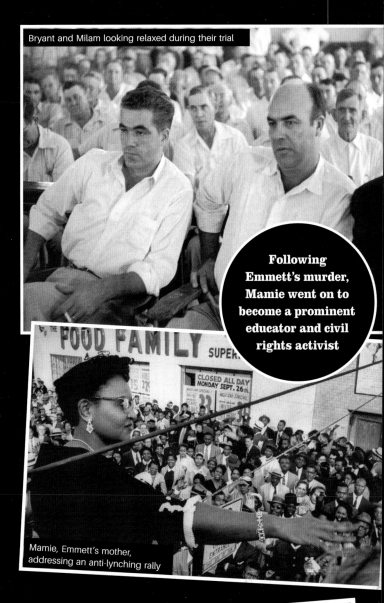

Bryant and Milam looking relaxed during their trial

Following Emmett's murder, Mamie went on to become a prominent educator and civil rights activist

Mamie, Emmett's mother, addressing an anti-lynching rally

CAROLYN BRYANT'S CONFESSION

The truth is that Emmett Till did little more than whistle at Carolyn Bryant – and may even have been whistling at a friend across the street and not at her at all. But whatever her reasons, Bryant testified that he grabbed her, verbally threatened her, and made lewd insinuations about his history with white women.

It took more than 50 years, but Bryant eventually admitted that she'd lied. Interviewed by author Timothy B. Tyson for his book, *The Blood of Emmett Till*, she finally broke her silence in 2007. "That part is not true," she said of the list of accusations she initially came up with. "Nothing that boy did could ever justify what happened to him." She went on to say that she also felt "tender sorrow" for Emmett's mother Mamie, and that the white supremacist segregation of her youth was wrong, although it had seemed normal at the time.

While she expressed regret, however, she didn't go quite so far as to apologise. The interview went public in 2017.

nisable corpse in an open casket. Newspaper photographs of the body shocked the entire country. Decent citizens of all colours and creeds were repulsed by the crime. Bryant and Milam could expect little support for their crime.

Except, they were acquitted. Five days in a sweltering segregated courtroom with an all-white jury meant the pair received an easy ride in the dock. Despite the evidence against them, and the testimonies of several witnesses – black people publicly accusing whites in court was a courageous act for the time – they walked from the courtroom free men. Some of the jurors later admitted that they didn't think the killing of a black man was worth a custodial or capital sentence. Immune from being tried twice for the same crime (under the 'double jeopardy' law), Bryant and Milam even admitted their guilt in a lucrative magazine interview not long afterwards. This act of hubris worked against them. Their infamy followed them wherever they tried to settle subsequently, and their businesses were boycotted and went bankrupt. After bleak lives marked by violence and petty crime, Milam died in 1980 and Bryant in 1994.

Till, meanwhile, lived on in people's imaginations, his death serving as the spark that ignited the Civil Rights Movement in earnest. The date of Emmett's murder, 28 August, was also the day in 1963 that Martin Luther King Jr. made his 'I Have A Dream' speech. And when the Reverend Jesse Jackson asked Rosa Parks why she refused to give up her bus seat to a white passenger that day in December 1955, she replied that she had considered moving to the back of the bus, but then "thought of

Emmett Till's grave in Illinois

"Despite their freedom, life for a young black family in the Deep South was extremely harsh"

Parks poses for a press image seated at the front of the bus, the space that was reserved for whites only

ROSA PARKS:
TIRED OF GIVING IN

A small act of defiance, caused by a community pushed too far, would be the catalyst for the nationwide Civil Rights Movement

When the Civil Rights Movement is mentioned, few people would fail to think of the woman who almost single-handedly kick-started the national movement: Rosa Parks. Many aspects of 1950s American society were strictly segregated and while Parks was not the first person who refused to obey the laws, she was the spark that lit the fire of civil rights throughout the land.

In what was just another day for Parks, riding home on the Montgomery city bus after work, she was asked to give up her designated seat to a white person. She refused, was arrested, and her court case gained the support of the local chapter of the National Association for the Advancement of Colored People (NAACP), who organised a citywide bus boycott that ran for 381 days. This nonviolent protest gained national coverage, acting as a catalyst to spread the Civil Rights Movement across the entire country, headed by the newly appointed head of the NAACP, Dr. Martin Luther King Jr.. To attribute this to the actions of a single person seems unfair but Parks' act of defiance is often seen as the straw that broke the camel's back. It was one injustice too far that inspired a large chunk of the US population to rise up and fight for equality.

Parks herself came from humble beginnings having been born in Tuskegee, a small town near the Alabama state capital Montgomery, on 4 February 1913. Her parents, Leona and James McCauley, a teacher and carpenter, valued education and were strong advocates of racial equality. Despite their freedom and strong views, life for a young black family in the Deep South was extremely harsh. The black community relied almost entirely on the white population for work, but the jobs were often menial and offered very little in the way of pay and perks.

Rosa grew up attending segregated schools, but was forced to drop out of high school at 16 to care for her sick grandmother and later her mother. She would return to school years later, encouraged by her husband, to gain her high school diploma. It is a testament to her will, and others sharing her plight, that despite her oppressive beginnings, she grew up with a great sense of self-worth. Those that knew her explained that she was softly spoken but carried with her a quiet strength and determination that saw her fight hard when challenged.

Parks found a job as a seamstress at a textile factory in Montgomery

and in 1932, aged 19, married Raymond Parks. Raymond, lacking a formal education of his own, was actively involved in the NAACP and Rosa would soon become involved as well. Her actions on 1 December 1955 reflect her passion for the cause, as she was not just a person who decided not to give up her seat, but a committed activist working to better the lives of black people in Alabama and throughout the United States.

The incident in December was, to many, a routine occurrence. Buses in Montgomery were segregated by colour, with the front reserved for white people and the back for black people. This meant that a black person would need to pay for their ticket at the front of the bus, get off and walk to the back door to find a seat. The bus drivers held ultimate authority in their vehicles, being able to move the segregation line back and force any black person to give up their seat in busy periods. Failure to do so would mean getting thrown off the bus and having the police called. Parks had already had a run-in with the driver, James Blake, a few years beforehand when Blake had driven off while Parks exited the bus to walk to the back doors.

> **Parks later stated that if she had realised that James Blake was the driver, she would never have got on the bus**

Parks, who had just finished a long shift, was seated on the crowded bus but in a row with three other black people. When Blake noticed a white man standing he ordered Parks and the others to give up their seats. While only one seat was needed, the law stated that whites and blacks couldn't be seated in the same row. The four at first refused, to which Blake replied, "You'd better make it light on yourselves and let me have those seats". While the others complied, Parks would not budge, stating that as she was not in the white section she didn't think she should have to give up her seat. When remembering the incident in later life, Parks said: "When that white driver stepped back toward us, when he waved his hand and ordered us up and out of our seats, I felt a determination to cover my body like a quilt on a winter night". With steely resolve, Parks refused to move an inch, forcing Blake to call his supervisor, asking for advice. The response was simple: "Well then, Jim, you do it, you got to exercise your powers and put her off, hear?" Parks was then arrested as she had technically broken the law by not giving up her seat. While she was being arrested, she asked the police officer a question: "Why do you push us around?" The question and response of "I don't know, but the law is the law," along with Parks' actions, are widely credited as one of

Parks, and other members of the boycott, would receive death threats for their actions

the catalysts for the Civil Rights Movement in America.

She was held in the police station for violating chapter 6, section 11 of the Montgomery city code that dealt with segregation. She was bailed out that evening by the president of the local NAACP chapter, Edgar Nixon. Nixon saw an opportunity to use Parks' arrest to further their cause and immediately began planning a boycott of the city's buses that night. The next day, the city was saturated with newspaper ads and over 35,000 handbills, produced the night before, were distributed around black neighbourhoods. The boycott called for all black people to avoid using the buses until they were treated with the

Edgar Nixon played an instrumental role in the bus boycott and bailed Rosa Parks out of jail

WOMEN OF THE CIVIL RIGHTS MOVEMENT

Fannie Lou Hamer
Having faced brutal beatings in jail campaigning for equal rights, Hamer spoke candidly of her experiences live on air in 1964, prompting President Lyndon B. Johnson to organise an impromptu press conference to draw media coverage away from this embarrassing insight into racist America. Hamer spoke of her terrible experiences at the 1964 Democratic conference.

Dorothy Height
President of the National Council for Negro Women for 40 years, Dorothy worked tirelessly to help low-income schools and provide for poor families. Her efforts led President Obama to describe her as the "godmother of the Civil Rights Movement" in 2010. Height is seen by many as one of the key figures of the Civil Rights Movement.

Daisy Bates
An iconic member of the civil rights campaign, Bates' most famous achievement was leading the Little Rock Nine to enrol in the Little Rock Central High School in 1957. After Little Rock, Bates worked tirelessly to improve living conditions in her poor community.

Septima Clark
With her work including securing equal pay for black teachers, Septima Clark was dubbed the "mother of the movement" by Martin Luther King Jr. and had been fighting for equality since 1919. Clark would continue her work with the SCLC until her retirement in 1970.

Bernice Robinson
Robinson was a civil rights activist who recognised the importance of education in the fight for equality. She helped set up Citizenship Schools in South Carolina and worked with the SCLC across the South to teach adult reading skills to help black Americans pass literacy tests in order to vote.

Diane Nash
As the founder of the Student Nonviolent Coordinating Committee (SNCC), Diane Nash was one of the most influential figures of the entire Civil Rights Movement. She helped organise sit-ins and the now legendary Freedom Riders. Nash worked tirelessly around Nashville and beyond to win equal rights and end segregation.

Parks became a figurehead for the Civil Rights Movement and continued to fight for equality throughout her life

The SCLC is still active today with Charles Steele Jr. the current president, a position previously held by Dr. King's daughter Bernice

same level of respect as white passengers while on board, the segregated seating was removed and black drivers were hired. The Montgomery Improvement Association (MIA) was formed to spearhead the initiative and at its head was Dr. Martin Luther King Jr., a recent newcomer to Montgomery and the man who saw a chance to use Parks' case to take the struggle nationwide.

Black taxi companies reduced their fares to the price of a bus ticket in support of the boycott

The first day of the boycott coincided with Parks' trial, where she was fined $14. Continuing for another 380 days, the boycott saw many black people shun the bus in favour of using black taxi companies, carpooling or simply walking to work – with some people walking up to 32 kilometres (20 miles) a day. It soon began to have the desired effect as the bus company's profits slumped, leading to much of the fleet sitting idle for over a year. The successes were tempered by the backlash, however, as black churches were burned and both King and Nixon's houses were attacked. The authorities also tried to break the boycott through other means, with the taxi companies that took black people to work having their insurance revoked and arrests made under antiquated anti-boycott laws.

These heavy-handed reactions did little to sway the MIA who went on the legal offensive. Only a year before, the Brown v Board of Education Supreme Court ruling had found that segregated schools were unconstitutional. Armed with this, their legal team sought to challenge the segregation laws for public transport. In June 1956 they were ruled unconstitutional and despite resistance the decision was upheld by the Supreme Court in November 1956. With the law on their side and both the bus company and city businesses suffering financial losses, the city had

FORMATION OF THE SCLC

The Southern Christian Leadership Conference (SCLC) was an organisation born out of the success of the Montgomery Bus Boycott. Headed by Martin Luther King Jr., the group sought to capitalise on the victory in Alabama and advance the cause of civil rights in a nonviolent manner. Black communities in the South at this time were formed around the church, so having a minister as the figurehead was an obvious choice. King himself stated, "The SCLC is church orientated because of the very structure of the Negro community in the South."

Combining various smaller civil rights groups under one spiritual umbrella, the SCLC formed three main goals which would be the bedrock of the organisation. The first was to encourage white Southerners to join their cause. Although a staggering amount of hate and vitriol was levelled against blacks in the South, the SCLC believed that not all people harboured racist views. All black people were also encouraged and asked to "seek justice and reject all injustice". The final and perhaps most important point for the group was a strict belief and adherence to nonviolent protest. The unofficial motto of the group became "not one hair of one head of one white person shall be harmed".

little choice but to end segregation on public transport. The boycott was formally ended on 20 December 1956.

Rosa Parks' resistance ignited one of the largest and most successful protests against racial segregation in the South. Its nonviolent means saw it gain national coverage and helped to send the struggle for civil rights nationwide.

Prior to the Montgomery Bus Boycott, African Americans were not hired as drivers, were forced to sit at the back of the bus and had to give up their seats to white passengers.

THE LITTLE ROCK NINE

In Little Rock, Arkansas in 1957, nine black students asserted their right to education in a racially mixed school. Their first day did not go smoothly

Along with the Montgomery Bus Boycott and the speeches of Martin Luther King Jr., one of the most resonant events of the African American struggle for civil rights took place in Little Rock, Arkansas in September 1957. In every other way, Central High School was unremarkable, but it became the site of a crucial test to Supreme Court legislation.

The beginnings of the story were in 1951, when 13 parents in Topeka, Kansas filed a lawsuit against their local board of education. In the Southern states of America at that time, racial segregation was mandated by law. The Topeka parents, with the encouragement and support of the National Association for the Advancement of Colored People (NAACP), called for the district to reverse this policy. The named plaintiff in the case was Oliver L. Brown, and the subsequent case was named Brown v Board of Education of Topeka. It turned out to be a landmark ruling: the US Supreme Court, taking the case along with other similar filings from South Carolina, Virginia, Washington and Delaware, concluded in May 1954 that having separate schools for white and black students was unconstitutional. It called for immediate desegregation and reintegration of black pupils into all-white schools. Problematically, however, it suggested no procedure by which this might be achieved.

In Arkansas, as elsewhere in the South, the school board largely accepted the ruling, took advice from the NAACP, and began planning for gradual reintegration, beginning in 1957 with its high schools. Undeterred by the vocal opposition of segregationist groups the Mothers' League of Central High School and the Capital Citizens' Council, nine students registered to be Central's first black students. They were Minnijean Brown, Elizabeth Eckford, Ernest Green, Thelma Mothershed, Melba Pattillo, Gloria Ray, Terrence Roberts, Jefferson Thomas, and Carlotta Walls. Their first day at school made national headlines, but not for the reasons they might have hoped. They arrived at the school gates to find state troopers pointing guns at them.

The Governor of Arkansas at the time was Orval Faubus. He was a Democrat who had actually gained office as a progressive candidate. By September of 1957, however, he was struggling in the polls, finding that he was being strongly challenged by opponents who thrived on stoking the prejudices of the local white voters. Apparently for reasons of self-interest then, Faubus sided with the segregationists of his constituency. On 2 September, he announced that he would be utilising the Arkansas National Guard to block the Nine's entry to Central High. He claimed that this was for their own protection, citing the possibility of violence if they were allowed to attend the school as planned.

The Nine did indeed encounter hostility other than that of the military: crowds of baying white protesters turned out to make sure that the Nine knew they were unwelcome. Eckford, who arrived separately from the other eight, underwent a particularly terrifying ordeal (left), surrounded, alone, by a hostile mob.

The events attracted national and international publicity, and after only three days of the standoff, President Dwight D Eisenhower was personally involved, threatening Faubus that "the Federal Constitution will be upheld by me by every legal means at my command." Faced with the ire of the president of the United States (not to mention possible jail time), Faubus became understandably conciliatory. On 14 September, he travelled to Newport, Rhode Island for a private conference with Eisenhower, the outcome of which saw Faubus agree to put aside his apparent personal views on segregation to comply with the Supreme Court's ruling. By 21 September, Eisenhower was able to release a statement confirming that the Governor was withdrawing his troops, and the Nine would be welcomed unopposed to Central High, with officers of the local law ensuring their safety.

But even then, the matter wasn't settled. Two days later, likely with the tacit approval of Faubus, another organised mob formed outside the school, of such a size that the police could not control it. Genuinely for their own safety this time, the Nine were sent home once again. Eisenhower removed the Arkansas National Guard from Faubus's control, and replaced them with troops from the 101st Airborne Division to enforce federal law. The Nine attended their first day of classes on 25 September.

Legal challenges to integration in Arkansas continued, however, and the Nine faced appalling hostility within Central High's walls: burned in effigy and on the receiving end of constant violent attacks. Brown retaliated, and was expelled for doing so. Green was ultimately the only one of the Nine to stick it out at Central High until graduation, although they all went on to distinguished careers. Green and Brown both went into politics, while Pattillo became a news reporter and broadcaster. The Nine all received personal invitations to attend President Barack Obama's inauguration ceremony in 2009.

President Bill Clinton awarded each of the Nine a Congressional Gold Medal in 1999 for outstanding service to the USA

Central High School
still exists, and is
now a historic site also
housing a Civil Rights
museum

LITTLE ROCK'S 'LOST YEAR'

Orval Faubus was not going to take interference in his state lightly, even from the US President himself. Despite apparently convivial talks intended to help diffuse the situation in Little Rock, the white protests against the black students were thought to be ongoing with Faubus's tacit - if not public - approval. And when Eisenhower sent in troops to decisively enforce federal law, Faubus took the extraordinary measure of shutting down all of Little Rock's high schools for the school year of 1958-59. The period has become known as Little Rock's 'Lost Year'.

Faubus's reasoning was that the imposition of federal troops beyond his control on Little Rock was a usurpation of power by central government. The peculiar situation saw teachers continuing to show up for work in empty classrooms while students of all races were barred from attending - although sports fixtures like football games were allowed to continue. Some students went to school in neighbouring counties, some went to work or joined the military, and many simply dropped out.

The Lost Year ended in June 1959, when federal courts declared the closures, like segregation, were unconstitutional. Public high schools reopened on 12 August 1959, with desegregation continuing slowly and black students still facing considerable discrimination.

Governor Orval E. Faubus

BUILDING A DREAM: THE RISE OF MLK

The long, hard road that led Martin Luther King Jr. from the segregated south to 'I Have a Dream' and the March on Washington

The history of the Civil Rights Movement is also the biography of Martin Luther King Jr. King was a leader at every major protest, from the inception of the civil rights campaign for legal equality in the Montgomery Bus Boycott of 1955 to the Poor People's Campaign of 1968, which marked civil rights' turn towards social and economic issues. King's 'I Have A Dream' speech, delivered in 1963 at the March on Washington, defined the Civil Rights Movement's struggle and its inspirations, the twinned promises of the Sermon on the Mount and the American Constitution. Nor, following his murder in April 1968, could the Civil Rights Movement find a leader to replace King's moral authority and popular appeal.

Yet the biography of Martin Luther King Jr. is more than the history of the Civil Rights Movement. King was a brilliant but troubled man — a preacher's son with doubts about Christ, and a family man drawn to adulterous affairs. King was born Michael King on 15 January 1929 in Atlanta, Georgia. His father, also Michael King, was a Baptist pastor. When Michael Jr. was two, Michael Sr. became leader of the Ebenezer Baptist Church, a prominent black church in Atlanta. In 1934, after attending the Fifth Baptist World Alliance Congress in Berlin, Michael King Sr. changed his and his son's forenames in honour of the Protestant reformer Martin Luther.

Along with his father's name, Martin Luther King Jr. inherited both his father's commitment to communal leadership through the black church, and also his related commitment to civil rights. Martin Luther King Sr. was a lifelong campaigner against Jim Crow laws. He had campaigned for equal pay for black teachers, and boycotted Atlanta's bus system because of attacks on black passengers. He was prominent in the Atlanta chapter of the National Association for the Advancement of Colored People (NAACP), and would eventually rise to its leadership.

As a boy, Martin Luther King Jr. saw how the churches were the moral leaders of Atlanta's black community. He also witnessed first-hand his father's refusal to accept racism. When father and son were sitting in a shoe store, they were asked to move to the rear of the store. King Sr. preferred to walk out. "I don't care how long I have to live under this system," Martin Jr. heard his father say, "I will never accept it." When a white policeman called King Sr. "boy", the pastor gestured to Martin Jr. and replied, "This is a boy. I'm a man. Until you call me one, I will not listen."

King Sr. was unrelenting in his determination to make a man of his young son. He sent Martin to do field work, so that he would understand something of the suffering of his ancestors. He beat Martin Jr. until the age of 15, and expected his son to follow him into the ministry. Martin Jr. was a child chorister at Ebenezer Baptist Church, and his mother, Alberta, was the organist. But Martin Jr, as he later admitted, had profound doubts about Christian doctrine; at 13, he denied the Resurrection of Jesus during a Sunday School class.

Still, Martin Jr. possessed the moral impulse that made a preacher, and the rhetorical ability that made a preacher a communal leader; at high school, Martin Jr. was a winning debater. He was also intelligent enough to skip two of the four grades of high school, and enter Atlanta's historically black Morehouse College at 15. Leaving Morehouse in 1947 at the age of 18 with a degree in sociology, Martin Jr. decided to train for the ministry at Crozer Theological Seminary in Pennsylvania.

At Morehouse, King had fallen in love with a white student, but friends had convinced him not to propose marriage, because an interracial union would damage his chances of obtaining the pastorship of a black church in the South. In 1953, King married Coretta Scott, a black woman from Alabama, in a ceremony on the lawn of his parents' house. In the following year, he obtained the pastorship of Dexter Avenue Baptist Church in Montgomery, Alabama. Meanwhile, he studied as a doctoral student of religion at Boston University. In 1991, an investigation would conclude that King had plagiarised significant portions of his doctoral thesis from the thesis of another student.

King found his public identity in 1955, as a leader of the year-long Montgomery Bus Boycott. The boycott campaign also demonstrated the risk involved in even peaceful protest. On the night of 30 January 1956, an unknown attacker threw a bomb onto the porch of the King house. Coretta King and a friend got out of the living room before the bomb exploded; King's infant daughter Yolanda was asleep in a back room.

In 1957, King co-founded the Southern Christian Leadership Conference (SCLC) with other leading activists including Fred Shuttlesworth and Ralph

> **MLK and George Washington are the only two Americans whose birthdays are now national holidays**

"I have a dream that one day this nation will rise up and live out the true meaning of its creed"

In 1958, King nearly died after being stabbed in the chest during a book reading by a mentally ill black woman

Washington DC, 28 August 1963: Martin Luther King Jr. delivers the 'I Have A Dream' speech

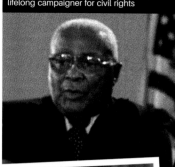

Dr. Martin Luther King Sr. (1897-1984), lifelong campaigner for civil rights

Between 1957 and 1968, King travelled more than 6 million miles, spoke on more than 2,500 occasions, and wrote five books

Ralph Abernathy (1926-1990), Baptist Minister, King's close ally, and co-founder of the Southern Christian Leadership Conference

Civil rights pioneer A Philip Randolph (1889-1979) became one of the leaders of the 1963 March on Washington

Abernathy, both of whom were Baptist ministers at Birmingham, Alabama; and Joseph Lowery, a minister at Mobile, Alabama.

As King and the SCLC leadership developed strategies for confronting the law without having to break it, and for using the moral authority of the church against the legal authority of the government, King drew upon a century of nonviolent protest.

At Morehouse, King had read Walter Rauschenbusch, a 19th-century Baptist proponent of the 'social gospel' – the idea that social problems could be solved by the application of Christian principles. More recently, he had witnessed the 'crusade' for moral reform by the white evangelist Billy Graham. King also knew Henry David Thoreau's 1849 essay 'Resistance to Civil Government', better known under its reprinted title, 'Civil Disobedience'. Leo Tolstoy had drawn on Thoreau and the Christian reformer Adin Ballou to develop a theory of Christian 'nonviolence'. Another of Tolstoy's readers, Mahatma Gandhi, had used 'passive resistance' to discredit the British Empire in India. King became the inheritor of this tradition.

At first, however, King's tactics were rebuffed. In December 1961, the SCLC gave its support to local campaigners for the desegregation of Albany, Georgia. When desegregationists peaceably moved into segregated spaces, the police made mass arrests. King, given a choice between a fine or jail, chose jail. He was released after a few days; the evangelical preacher Billy Graham paid King's fine. The Albany protests faltered, and the coalition between the SCLC and the local campaigners broke up.

Albany taught King that it was not enough to break the law. Like Gandhi's campaigns against the salt tax, the SCLC must confront the authorities by occupying public spaces with crowds, and then force a crisis that would disgrace the authorities, by revealing them as defenders

CORETTA SCOTT KING

Martin Luther King Jr's wife Coretta Scott was born at Marion, Alabama in 1927; her father's grandmother Delia Scott, an ex-slave, was the midwife. During the Depression, the Scott children helped support their family by picking cotton. As Marion's high school was segregated, Scott's mother, who had not been formally educated, drove Scott and the other black teenagers to the nearest high school. She and her sister became the first black undergraduates at Antioch College, Ohio. There, Scott studied music and entered the struggle for civil rights.

In 1951, Scott won a scholarship to study at the New England Conservatory of Music in Boston. That winter, a mutual friend introduced her to Martin Luther King Jr. Despite his parents' initial suspicion, they married in June 1953. When King secured a position as a pastor, Scott, already pregnant with the first of their four children, had to abandon plans for a singing career. Instead, as the Montgomery Bus Boycott placed her husband at the centre of the Civil Rights struggle, she joined him as a campaigner. Their marriage survived his infidelities and harassment by the FBI, which included mailing her a tape of her husband committing adultery.

After King's assassination, Coretta Scott King continued to campaign for civil rights and peace

President Johnson receives King at the White House in December 1963

of unjust laws. In April 1963, King and the SCLC applied this insight to the effort to desegregate Birmingham, Alabama. Television cameras filmed the reaction in Birmingham. The police used tear gas, dogs and water cannons against unarmed civilians, some of them children. Such sights pushed white Americans to decide whether they could still tolerate Jim Crow laws. A majority could not.

Arrested in Birmingham, King was now the face of the SCLC. While the FBI wiretapped King and searched for communist sympathies among his associates, and while rival black groups like the Nation of Islam and the separatists who shortly afterwards formed the Black Panthers advocated violence against whites, King was determined to present the struggle for civil rights as an American struggle. In August 1963, he succeeded, delivering his 'I Have A Dream' speech to an estimated 250,000 marchers, most of them black, after the March on Washington for Jobs and Freedom. A year later, Congress passed the Civil Rights Act of 1964.

However, the March on Washington for Jobs and Freedom was not King's idea, and the SCLC was only one of the 'Big Six' civil rights groups who organised the march. The march was the dream of two veteran campaigners, A Philip Randolph, the founder of the Leadership Conference on Civil Rights (LCCR), and Bayard Rustin. In 1941, Randolph and Rustin, both of whom were socialists and admirers of Gandhi's nonviolence, and the Dutch-born white clergyman A.J. Muste, had planned a march on Washington to protest segregation in war

> *"Such sights pushed white Americans to decide whether they could still tolerate Jim Crow laws. A majority could not"*

BAYARD RUSTIN: FORGOTTEN HERO

Born in Pennsylvania in 1912 and raised a Quaker, Bayard Rustin was a lifelong fighter for civil rights, and the organiser of the March on Washington. Yet his evolving political opinions and his homosexuality meant that his fellow civil rights leaders were wary of associating too closely with him.

Rustin's activism began in the late 1930s, when he was working as a nightclub singer in New York City and an active member of the Communist Party. In World War II, he became a conscientious objector and a member of the Socialist Party. In 1941, he planned an anti-segregation march on Washington with A Philip Randolph and A.J. Muste. In 1942, 13 years before the Montgomery Bus Boycott, Rustin was arrested and beaten by police at Louisville, Kentucky after refusing to move to the back of a bus.

In 1947, Rustin took part in the first of the Freedom Rides, the organised disruption of interstate bus services. In 1948, he travelled to India and studied Gandhi's tactics of nonviolence. In 1956, it was Rustin who persuaded Martin Luther King to abandon his armed bodyguards.

The end of Rustin's long political journey in neoconservatism and campaigns for gay rights ensured his exclusion from mainstream black politics. He died in 1987 – and received a posthumous Presidential Medal of Freedom in 2013.

Bayard Rustin (left) and the labour organiser Cleveland Robinson, 28 August 1963

King was jailed 29 times during the civil rights campaign, including for driving at 30mph in a 25mph zone

production and the US military. President Roosevelt had received the trio at the White House, and to pre-empt the march, had issued an executive order to desegregate war production – but not the military.

In 1957, Randolph and Rustin had organised the Prayer Pilgrimage for Freedom with King, who had spoken before an estimated 25,000 protesters in Washington. Randolph, who pioneered the use of 'prayer protests', also directed Rustin to mentor King on strategies of nonviolence. If the 1963 March on Washington was the realisation of Randolph and Rustin's dream of mass protest, King's speech at the Washington Mall was the realisation of its means, the appearance on the national stage of a charismatic speaker whose blend of moral gravity and emotional intensity could move the hearts as well as the consciences of the white majority.

THE POWER OF NONVIOLENT PROTEST

The Civil Rights Movement in America sought to break down the social barriers of segregation by championing nonviolent and passive resistance in the face of terrible brutality and hate

Hate begets hate; violence begets violence; toughness begets a greater toughness. We must meet the forces of hate with the power of love... Our aim must never be to defeat or humiliate the white man, but to win his friendship and understanding." These words from Dr. Martin Luther King Jr. eloquently summed up the intentions of the majority of civil rights campaigners in America; namely, that their goal of equality was to be met through nonviolent and peaceful protest, a stark contrast to the violence and hate levelled against black communities over the previous few centuries. One of the crowning achievements of the movement was its effectiveness in promoting these ideals and affecting real change in the country while hardly ever raising a hand in anger.

"Love thy neighbour" was a biblical verse that King took to heart. He, and other activists, believed that love was the force that would win equality and end the racist and segregated laws that infested the USA. Love in their mind didn't have to be a literal, emotional bond, but a powerful force that could be used for good.

The 20th century had revealed just how effective mankind had become in waging war, with his violent tendencies playing out through a multitude of wars, genocides and civil inequality, backed up by brutal repression. In contrast, there was also a rise in peaceful, nonviolent protest that sought to enforce positive change without the need for bloodshed. The genesis of nonviolent protest in the American Civil Rights Movement lay in King's teachings and actions.

One of the biggest influences on King's philosophy came not from what was happening in America, but rather from actions that occurred on the other side of the world. Mahatma Gandhi, the driving force behind India's independence from the British Empire, had championed nonviolent protest as a way to fight oppression and win his people's freedom. In King's own words, Gandhi was the person who had the most influence on the actions he took during the struggle to gain civil rights for black people in America. Having heard of Gandhi's work from his training as a minister, King became deeply influenced by the Indian activist's teachings after hearing an old university professor talk about his experiences shortly after visiting the country. King did not expect that his interest in Gandhi's work would ever have practical application in his life, never mind forming the core of his ideals and actions during the Civil Rights Movement.

The major practitioners of nonviolent resistance were beginning to communicate directly and share their philosophy. Gandhi and Leo Tolstoy were in correspondence

and once the American movement got off the ground, King began to add his own thoughts to the mix. In 1959, King travelled to India in order to learn more of how the independence movement had operated. After the visit, he was "more convinced than ever before that the method of nonviolent resistance is the most potent weapon available to oppressed people in their struggle for justice and human dignity".

The Civil Rights Movement had already made successful use of nonviolent protest in the Montgomery Bus Boycott, which had proved the effectiveness of this passive form of protest. King and the other leaders of the movement met hate with love in their efforts to dismantle the institutionalised racism, inequality and discrimination that came with segregation. Many years of Jim Crow laws had shown that those who supported segregation would go to any lengths to maintain the status quo and keep control over the black population.

A burnt-out Freedom Rider bus. Its passengers were targeted for simply travelling from state to state

Over ten interstate Freedom Rides took place between May and December in 1961

The goal of the resistance was an end to segregation, and one of the ways to achieve that was to ensure that the long history of violence used against the black community in the South was shown to the world. Two organisations that were created following the success of the bus boycott were the Student Nonviolent Coordinating Committee (SNCC) and the Congress of Racial Equality (CORE). Both of these groups were made up primarily of students who had been inspired by a conference in April 1960 sponsored by King. They hoped to use the momentum gained by the actions in Montgomery to drive the cause nationwide. The students were looking for a way to have their actions directly impact people's lives without being detrimental to their cause.

The sit-in movement, first making national headlines on 2 February 1960, in Greensboro, North Carolina, was started by four college students. During the lunchtime rush, the four students sat in the white-only designated seating at the lunch counter and were refused service. Instead of leaving, they quietly waited to be served. The store was chosen specifically as the Woolworth chain was known throughout the country and the demonstrators wanted a location that clearly separated people based on colour alone. The men wanted to highlight the hypocrisy of a store that would accept their money while buying school supplies but wouldn't have them sitting at the lunch counter.

The Greensboro Four, as they became known, vowed that they would continue this protest and in greater numbers. With more and more volunteers joining them, they worked in shifts to stay at the counter

Many Jim Crow laws were finally repealed in 1964 with the signing of the Civil Rights Act

all day, simply waiting for service. These actions often made these men and women the targets of abuse, and they were shouted at, pelted with food or drink, threatened, beaten or forcibly removed. Never responding in anger, the protesters were usually arrested and as they were escorted out, a new group would be ready to take their place.

Sit-ins had been used since the 1940s, and were now an integral part of the nonviolent protest in the Civil Rights Movement. When the media

Dr. King, seen here with his wife and Indian Prime Minister Jawaharlal Nehru, was convinced of the power of nonviolent protest after a visit to India in 1959

Freedom Riders are attacked by a mob in Birmingham, Alabama. This image was seen worldwide and received massive condemnation

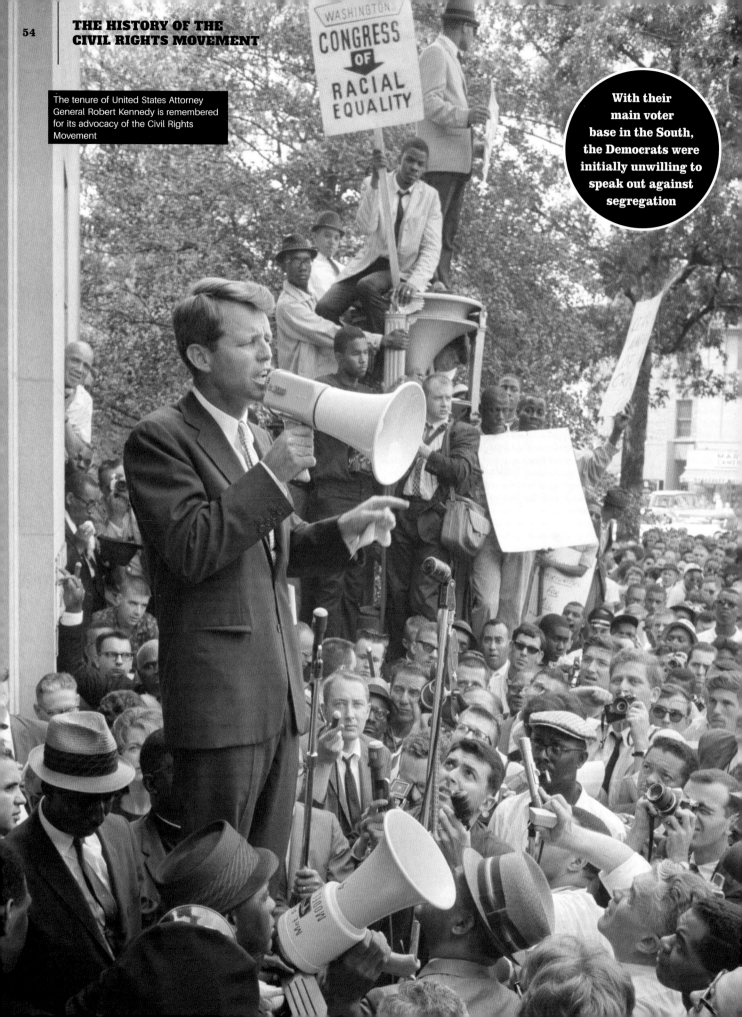

The tenure of United States Attorney General Robert Kennedy is remembered for its advocacy of the Civil Rights Movement

WASHINGTON
CONGRESS
OF
RACIAL
EQUALITY

With their main voter base in the South, the Democrats were initially unwilling to speak out against segregation

got wind of the protests, they quickly spread across the South, taking 54 cities' lunch counters by storm. Six months after the initial protest, the store finally pulled its segregated counters, allowing people of any colour to eat free from molestation. These protests aimed to highlight the inequality and hit a store's finances; if their seats were filled with protesters not being served, this would drastically reduce the income from the lunch rush. This simple and passive form of protest was extremely effective and brought the ugly face of American segregation into the national consciousness.

Following the sit-ins, Freedom Riders were an example of a hopeful, and some think naive, form of nonviolent protest that gained traction in the early 1960s. Its participants were made up of both black and white activists who were organised by CORE. Their objective was simple – to travel from Washington, DC to the Deep South in small groups via bus to periodically break the strict segregation laws on the way. Their objective was to raise awareness of these laws and discover and showcase which towns and cities actively supported the Jim Crow laws. The timetable planned for a two-week trip through the Southern states to arrive in New Orleans on 17 May 1961, the anniversary of the historic Brown v Board of Education ruling. This plan was a controversial one, with even members of the Civil Rights Movement thinking it was too confrontational. Segregation was a fact of life in the South and the entire post-Civil War culture was built on its foundations. White segregationists would and did view it as an attack on their very way of life. There was a very real possibility that the Freedom Riders would be arrested, attacked or even killed as they made their way to New Orleans.

The Riders had their trail laid for them by a woman named Irene Morgan. In the 1940s, she successfully fought against segregation on interstate buses, much like Rosa Parks had fought against segregated city buses in Montgomery a decade later. Unfortunately, the Southern states overruled this federal law by enforcing the segregation that existed in the Southern state laws. The Riders were not sent in without instruction, however, and received training in Washington, DC on how to deal with confrontation and the inevitable violence they would encounter. The riders were even warned by King in Atlanta that the KKK were planning a welcoming committee for the buses in Alabama and encouraged the Riders to turn back. The buses were heckled, stopped, attacked and one set on fire as they entered Alabama. Local police forces, along with the FBI, were also turning a blind eye to planned KKK attacks on the Riders. The Klan was given 15 minutes without any police intervention and the sickening pictures taken of the mass brawl that ensued were widely circulated around the world. In this way, the Freedom Riders had achieved their objective: for the simple act of riding on a bus, they had almost been killed by mobs of locals and had embarrassed the USA – a country that prided itself on civil liberties – on the world stage. Even so, the Riders became stranded in Birmingham when the bus drivers refused to drive them any further. After a tense standoff in the airport, the government had to intervene to fly the battered and bruised Riders down to New Orleans.

> *" For the simple act of riding on a bus, they had almost been killed by mobs of locals "*

The Nation of Islam, an organisation that Malcolm X was once part of, called for a separate black US nation

The next chapter of the Freedom Ride is one of the best examples of what the nonviolent protest stood for. A second wave of Freedom Riders was on its way from Nashville to Birmingham, and the feeling was that if the ride stopped now, it would prove that segregation could be upheld by brutal violence. This second wave of riders knew the danger they were putting themselves in, and went so far as to write up their wills the night before they departed. By 17 May, pressure from the Kennedy administration, who had been scrambling to defuse the situation since the worldwide backlash, granted the Freedom Riders full police protection. This came none too soon as tensions in Birmingham between the Riders and the KKK had reached breaking point. This police presence disappeared as soon as the bus hit the Montgomery city limits, and the Riders and accompanying journalists were again subjected to horrific beatings.

A man undergoes tolerance training by having smoke blown in his face to prepare for a sit-in demonstration

PREPARE FOR THE WORST

When meeting aggression with pacifism, it may seem like training would be slightly redundant, but the Civil Rights Movement offered its activists two kinds of nonviolent training. Philosophical training aimed to shape a person's attitude and mental response to violence, whereas practical training gave demonstrators tips on how to organise and lead peaceful demonstrations. It also covered the basics of how to respond to physical attacks and protect oneself from serious injury or even death. As activists, and especially the Freedom Riders, saw, they could be subjected to anything from physical blows with fists, feet or objects to getting spat on, ran over or stabbed.

Training sessions would consist of role play, where members would experience being insulted, threatened or attacked in a controlled environment. The training helped to form a sense of camaraderie among groups of activists and while the training was taken seriously, many believed they would never have to put it to use. The first Freedom Rider volunteers were convinced that they wouldn't need to use their physical training, but soon found out they would have to employ this vital knowledge on a daily basis as they travelled south.

Participants in training sessions were required to first have a very serious and committed attitude to the cause. Calm confidence was thought to be the best defence in the face of aggression. With training came discipline, and the goal was to present an organised, unbreakable front that would absorb violence and be able to continue the protest regardless, rendering the opponents' force worthless.

After years of peaceful resistance, the Civil Rights Movement had many of the Jim Crow laws abolished in 1964 with the Civil Rights Act

King again intervened for the Riders, this time asking an armed mob of black taxi drivers, who had formed up to protect them, to stand down for fear that they would escalate the situation even further. The group's total dedication to nonviolent protest, even in the face of death, showed the commitment and bravery of all involved. The Riders' actions were starting to see results on a national level. The governors of Mississippi and Alabama relented to give the Riders the protection of the state police and National Guard under the guarantee that the Riders could be arrested for breaking the segregation laws once they arrived at a bus depot. The level of arrests soon led to overpopulation of the local prisons and President Kennedy called for a "cooling off" period. Ignoring his request, the Freedom Rides continued and were met with the same level of hate and violence wherever they went. By November 1961, six months after the first group departed from Washington, DC, the segregation laws, including separate toilet facilities and waiting rooms, were removed from all bus terminals in the US, while passengers were permitted to sit wherever they pleased on interstate buses and trains. The ride, which had originally been planned as a 14-day excursion, had been drawn out over many months and gained worldwide news coverage. The violence was condemned at every turn and the actions of

the Freedom Riders helped greatly to showcase the rampant inequality in the USA and show the power of peaceful, nonviolent protest.

The policy of "love thy neighbour" and pacifism shown in all circumstances was not accepted by all of the Civil Rights Movement or the black community. Some leaders thought that nonviolent protest was only adopted because of the overwhelming force of the opposition. There was no way black communities could go toe-to-toe with local police departments or hate groups like the KKK and come out on top. Community leaders like Malcolm X saw King's pacifism as leaving black people defenceless against white aggression. He even went so far as to call King a modern-day 'Uncle Tom', a derogatory and antiquated term used to describe a black person who sided with their white oppressors against other black people. Malcolm X and others who agreed with his more violent approach to combating segregation could not comprehend a nonviolent approach, when black communities had so frequently been the target of state-sanctioned violence and discrimination. Despite his powerful rhetoric, there is a school of thought that believes leaders like Malcolm X incited or condoned violence in order to make the peaceful protests stand out more. Segregationists would be more willing to work with a moderate like Dr.

Both King and Malcolm X were assassinated, King by a white supremacist and the latter by Nation of Islam members

John Lewis, one of the original group of 13 Freedom Riders, was elected to the US House of Representatives in 1986

King and Malcolm X may have had differing views, but were both passionate and committed activists

LOVE OVER HATE

Martin Luther King Jr. and the Civil Rights Movement as a whole, were influenced by other international peace protests and leaders. Dr. King was outspoken in his influence by and agreement with Indian peace activist Mahatma Gandhi, and the writings of author and spiritual pioneer Leo Tolstoy. Gandhi and Tolstoy began discussing the nature of nonviolent protest in a series of letters after the Indian activist asked for permission to print one of the author's letters in his South African newspaper, where he was stationed at the time. The letter, called 'A Letter to a Hindu', sparked a passionate correspondence that would continue until Tolstoy's death. In these letters, they discuss how violence seems unnatural for the human spirit and advocate for the return to the most basic natural state for a human: love. All three men, especially Gandhi and King, saw love as the driving factor that could end oppression and was the only answer to violence. Both Gandhi and King agreed that meeting violence and hate with love was not a sign of weakness, but rather of strength and didn't have to refer to feelings or sentiment but rather a powerful force that could be used for good. Taking both the teachings of Tolstoy and Gandhi, King said, "Power at its best is love implementing the demands of justice, and justice at its best is power correcting everything that stands against love," and sought to break down the barriers that he saw society had placed on the combining of love and power.

King when faced with the alternative of Malcolm X and organisations like the Black Panthers.

Being targeted by the authorities and organisations like the KKK, black communities took their protection into their own hands. This need led to groups like the Deacons for Defense and Justice being formed in 1964. Mostly made up of veterans from World War II and the Korean War, the Deacons provided armed guards to protect the homes and residences of activists. It was one of the first self-defence forces to make itself known in the Civil Rights Movement, and its creation was met with scepticism by the nonviolent majority, who either stayed silent over its actions or spoke out against them. Despite the resistance against them from both camps, the Deacons were effective in curbing KKK activities and violence against black communities, and providing security for the March Against Fear that occurred in Tennessee and Mississippi in 1966. Other communities also found that displays of force or the threat of violence were enough to stop attacks by the KKK and protect their families.

The Civil Rights Movement contained a fluid spectrum of thoughts and opinions, but mostly focused on nonviolent practices. These were the actions that saw the most positive change in both society and law. While it did not end the struggle for equality, it proved that love, bravery and determination could win out over hate and violence.

One of the letters Gandhi sent to Tolstoy from his residence in Johannesburg

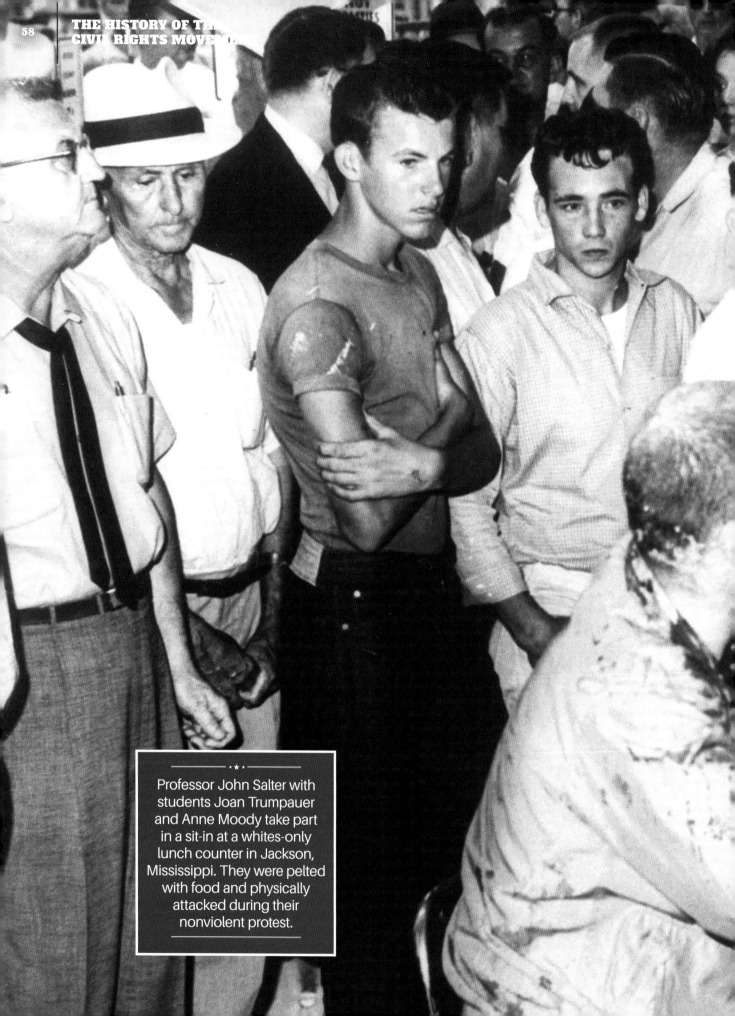

Professor John Salter with students Joan Trumpauer and Anne Moody take part in a sit-in at a whites-only lunch counter in Jackson, Mississippi. They were pelted with food and physically attacked during their nonviolent protest.

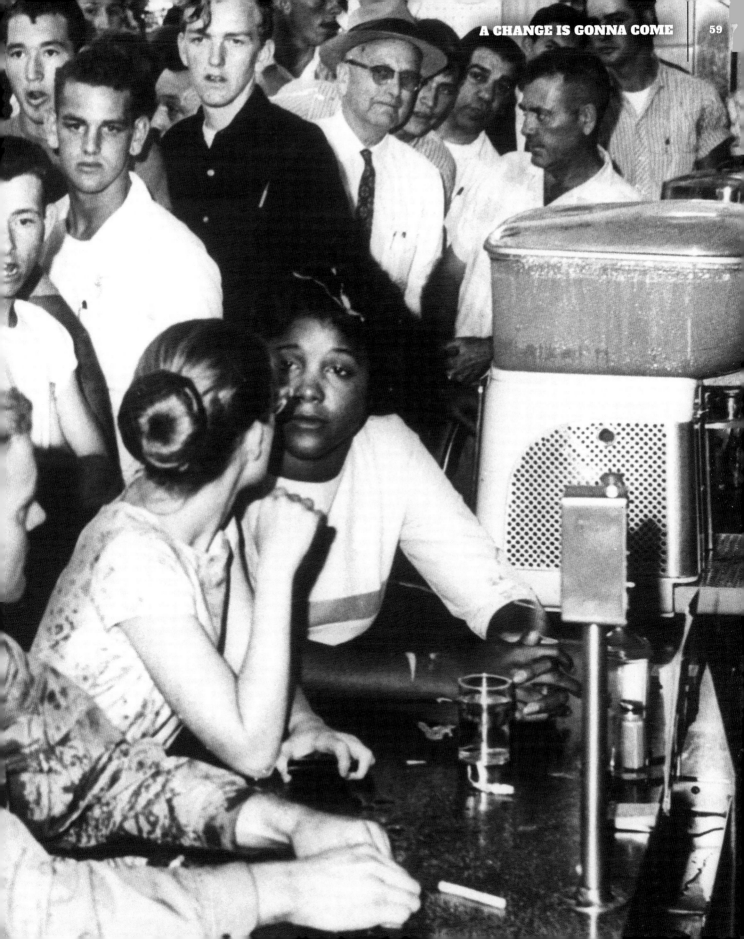

THE CAMPAIGN THAT
CHANGED
AMERICA

"The city government was firmly committed to racial segregation"

Many attempts were made to intimidate Reverend Shuttlesworth, but he refused to back down on his demands

Black protesters kneel before city hall, Birmingham, Alabama, minutes before being arrested for parading without a permit, 6 April 1963

Prior to the Birmingham Campaign, the Civil Rights Movement had begun to flounder in the face of black apathy and white indifference. The Albany Movement of late 1961 and 1962 had largely failed in the face of careful policing that employed the movement's own principle of nonviolence. But after the Birmingham Campaign, what had been a largely ignored regional protest commanded national and international attention. The city of Birmingham, Alabama, was where everything changed.

In 1963, Birmingham was one of the most segregated cities in the United States. Although the population was 40 per cent black, no black people were employed in department stores, as bus drivers, or worked for the fire department or police force. The only employment available to them, outside of black neighbourhoods, was manual labour or working as a house servant. The city's downtown shopping area was also rigidly segregated, with 'whites-only' counters and toilets, separate circles for blacks in movie theatres, and so on. The city government was firmly committed to racial segregation: when the courts overturned the requirement that the city's parks be segregated, the city authorities closed the parks.

It was against this background that Reverend Fred Shuttlesworth, pastor of the Bethel Baptist Church from 1953 to 1961, asked the Southern Christian Leadership Conference (SCLC) to come to Birmingham to help the boycott he was organising locally against segregated businesses. As Shuttlesworth said, "If you win in Birmingham, as Birmingham goes, so goes the nation."

The joint campaign began on 3 April 1963 with sit-ins at downtown whites-only lunch counters. Martin Luther King Jr. and the SCLC had learned from past mistakes to narrow their aims: rather than desegregate the whole city, they wanted to apply economic boycotts and nonviolent protests at the city's downtown businesses in the hope that local businessmen would then persuade the city authorities to change their opposition to desegregation. To that end, they organised an economic boycott of downtown businesses and, in response, some business owners began taking down their 'white only' notices. However, the city authorities, and in particular the Commissioner for Public Safety, Eugene 'Bull' Connor, fought back, cutting a food programme and warning businesses that had desegregated that they would lose their licences to trade.

The SCLC knew that they needed to gain national attention for their campaign and, in 'Bull' Connor, they were confident they had found the man who would bring them that attention. A dedicated segregationist, Connor was not a man to back down from a fight. When Klansmen beat up Freedom Riders in 1961, Connor made sure the police didn't arrive until the perpetrators had escaped. As he said to the press, "We are not going to stand for this in Birmingham. And if necessary we will fill the jail full and we don't care whose toes we step on."

That was what King and the SCLC were counting on. They increased the nonviolent protests, with marches, kneel-ins at segregated churches, and sit-ins at libraries and lunch counters. The aim was to fill the city's jails with so many protestors that the governmental machinery would grind to a halt. But much of the local black community was apathetic, while sections of local black leadership were openly hostile, convinced that

THE LETTER FROM A JAIL CELL

While he was being held in solitary confinement in jail, Martin Luther King Jr. read a copy of a newspaper, dated 12 April, which contained an open letter from eight white clergymen, entitled 'A Call for Unity', which criticised protests "directed and led in part by outsiders". King formulated a reply, writing first on the margins of the paper, then on scraps of paper and finally finished on a pad supplied by his lawyer. The reply, which became known as the 'Letter from Birmingham Jail', sought to explain and justify the principles and practice of nonviolent protest in the face of entrenched injustice - it is King's longest and most sustained exploration of the beliefs that motivated him and the way in which he sought to apply them. To answer the charge that he was an outsider stirring trouble in Birmingham, King wrote that he had been invited to join the protests and that "injustice anywhere is a threat to justice everywhere. We are caught in an inescapable network of mutuality, tied in a single garment of destiny. Whatever affects one directly, affects all indirectly." To answer the charge that he was an extremist, King pointed out that Jesus himself had been seen as an extremist. "So the question is not whether we will be extremists, but what kind of extremists we will be. Will we be extremists for hate or for love?" King's colleagues edited together the letter as it was smuggled out to them, and portions of it were published on 19 May 1963 in the *New York Post Sunday Magazine*.

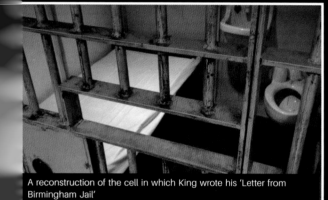

A reconstruction of the cell in which King wrote his 'Letter from Birmingham Jail'

the campaign would only inflame passions when Connor was due to retire from office soon.

On 10 April, the city authorities obtained a court order against the protests and began arresting protesters. The protest leaders decided to defy the injunction, but they were running desperately short of funds with which to bail the arrested campaigners. Some of the other leaders suggested that Martin Luther King Jr., as the main fundraiser for the campaign, should leave Birmingham to tour the country raising funds so that bail could be posted and those arrested, released. After prayer alone in his room, King said, "I don't know what will happen; I don't know where the money will come from. But I have to make a faith act."

On 12 April, Good Friday 1963, King led a protest march and was arrested and held in solitary confinement. While in jail, he wrote his famous 'Letter from Birmingham Jail'. King was held in prison until 20 April.

The arrest (his 13th) and imprisonment of Martin Luther King Jr. had drawn national attention and even the president, John F. Kennedy, had become involved. But to maintain the attention, the SCLC had to increase the pressure on the city's authorities. To that end, they decided to up the stakes, and offer the most innocent members of their movement as agents of nonviolent protest: the children would march.

James Bevel, an SCLC organiser, had proposed the idea and, after much hesitation, King had approved it. Many local black families were chary of the economic consequences of losing the family breadwinner to jail if they took part in the protests. But Bevel was confident that local students were ready and willing to take on the mantle of nonviolent protest, particularly after he ran workshops for them, including how to overcome the all-too-real fear of police dogs. Soon, these students would face these fears for real.

On 2 May, more than a thousand young black people, who had congregated at the 16th Street Baptist Church, began a march, a 'Children's Crusade', into downtown Birmingham in defiance of the city authorities and court injunctions. 'Bull' Connor was caught off guard by the

"Students were ready and willing to take on the mantle of nonviolent protest"

African Americans are attacked by dogs and water cannons during a protest against segregation

'Bull' Connor unwittingly did more to advance black civil rights than most people

size of the protest, and ordered the police to make mass arrests: over 600 were taken to jail. The city's jails were now overflowing.

What was more, national media had gathered in Birmingham to cover the extraordinary events. A more level-headed man might have taken cognisance of this, but not Connor. When, the next day, another thousand young people began to march towards the downtown, Connor ordered water cannons be turned on the marchers. These were high-pressure hoses, powerful enough to knock people flying and flay skin from flesh. Then, when bystanders called out against these tactics, Connor ordered that police dogs be sent in. The waiting photographers captured searing images of German shepherd dogs attacking young black people who, true to the principles of nonviolence, made no move to protect themselves, while reporters wired stories of the unrest to the national press. Birmingham had become front-page news.

Seeing the way their children had been treated, the local black community rallied behind the protests, which continued during the following week until the jails were so full that the enclosures at the state fairground were turned into holding pens. Business in downtown Birmingham had come to a complete halt. On 8 May, business leaders agreed to desegregate. And on 10 May, the city authorities finally caved in, agreeing to bring an end to segregated toilets, drinking fountains and lunch counters, the release on bail of the protesters held in jail, and a plan to increase black employment.

The response from die-hard segregationists was violent, including bombs aimed at killing King and SCLC leadership, and in reality, the city authorities dragged their feet in implementing the agreement. But the Birmingham Campaign had succeeded in convincing President Kennedy that civil rights could no longer be left at state level. On 11 June 1963, the president called for legislation to protect the rights of every American, regardless of race or religion. This would become the Civil Rights Act of 1964, the landmark legislation that outlawed discrimination, and it was signed into law by President Lyndon Johnson on 2 July 1964. The Birmingham Campaign had triumphed.

African American protesters, seen through a paddy wagon window, sing and pray during a protest at Birmingham Jail

Speaking to his wife from jail, King was careful in what he said, fearing the phone was bugged. It was

The mugshot of Martin Luther K Jr. taken after his arrest on 12 A

THE MAKING OF AN ICON

The single most iconic photograph of the Birmingham protests, run across three columns on the front page of the *New York Times* on 4 May 1963, shows a young black lad being attacked by a vicious police dog as a police officer holds the boy immobile. The boy himself, in an attitude of calm indifference, seems to personify the ideals of nonviolent protest. That's what the photo appears to show. But it turns out that the photo was not what it seemed. The boy in the photo, Walter Gadsden, wasn't even part of the protest but had bunked school and wanted to see what was going on. Moreover, Gadsden, when interviewed, has stated that rather than the police officer attacking him, he was trying to hold the dog back. When Gadsden's parents saw the picture in the paper the next day, they were appalled that their son had missed class. Gadsden was, nevertheless, arrested: the photo, taken by Bill Hudson, made him the unwitting face of the Birmingham Campaign.

When King was arrested, his wife, Coretta, had just given birth to their fourth child, Bernice

On 11 May, segregationists planted a bomb in the motel where King and other leaders of the SCLC had been staying

The iconic image of the Birmingham Campaign is not quite what it seems

───── ★★★ ─────
Firemen turn their firehoses on a group of young civil rights protesters during the Birmingham Campaign on the orders of the city's commissioner of public safety 'Bull' Connor.

I HAVE A DREAM

22 November 1963

THE ASSASSINATION OF JFK

Jackie Kennedy's blood-stained pink suit lies in the National Archives and will not be displayed until at least 2103

By November 1963, John F. Kennedy had fast become one of the most progressive presidents to ever hold office. In the months prior to his fateful trip to Dallas, JFK had conducted his famous Civil Rights Address to the nation and had begun the legislative machinations that would lead to the Civil Rights Act. His speech had taken the fight for equal rights from a lawful standpoint to a moral imperative that the United States had a responsibility to address. With the president himself showing outright support, the Civil Rights Movement finally had real momentum.

So when former US marine Lee Harvey Oswald fired his rifle at the presidential motorcade at 12.30pm, he sent a shockwave through the nation, the Civil Rights Movement and the world at large. The country was rocked as one as news spread of the shooting and the subsequent news of JFK's death upon arrival at a nearby hospital hit the headlines. Traffic ground to a halt, schools were dismissed and every American ran to every radio or television set they could find. Much like the Pearl Harbor attack before it and the 9/11 catastrophe that would follow decades later, JFK's murder became a flashpoint in American history.

Oswald himself would be fatally shot just two days later, but that wouldn't stop the sheer impact that the President's assassination would have on the Civil Rights Movement. His successor, Lyndon B. Johnson, was even more committed to pushing through the act than JFK, and while he wasn't as skilled at dealing with Congress as Kennedy had been, he ensured that the new laws entered the Constitution. The fight for civil rights could have been derailed by the murder, but instead JFK's shocking death calcified the movement as it marched towards true equality for African Americans.

Though it has become an anchor for conspiracy theories, an investigation into the assassination concluded that Lee Harvey Oswald acted alone

• Birmingham, Alabama schools integrated
10 September 1963

By September 1963, 144 school districts across the United States had begun the slow process of desegregation. However, not every state was willing. The governor of Alabama, George Wallace, had ordered state patrolmen to block the doors of Birmingham schools, effectively stopping black students from entering. The government had to step in so that desegregation could finally begin.

• The Civil Rights Act 1964

Following the assassination of JFK in November 1963, leaders of the Civil Rights Movement feared their fight for equality would be derailed. However, the shock loss of the president and the support of Lyndon B. Johnson saw a new addition to US law – the Civil Rights Act – come into full effect in the summer of 1964.

• MLK wins Nobel Peace Prize
14 October 1964

In 1964, more than a year after the March on Washington and his iconic 'I Have a Dream' speech, Martin Luther King Jr. was awarded the Nobel Peace Prize in recognition of his nonviolent efforts to gain civil rights for African Americans. The award, which arrived in the same year as the Civil Rights Act, helped solidify MLK's growing persona.

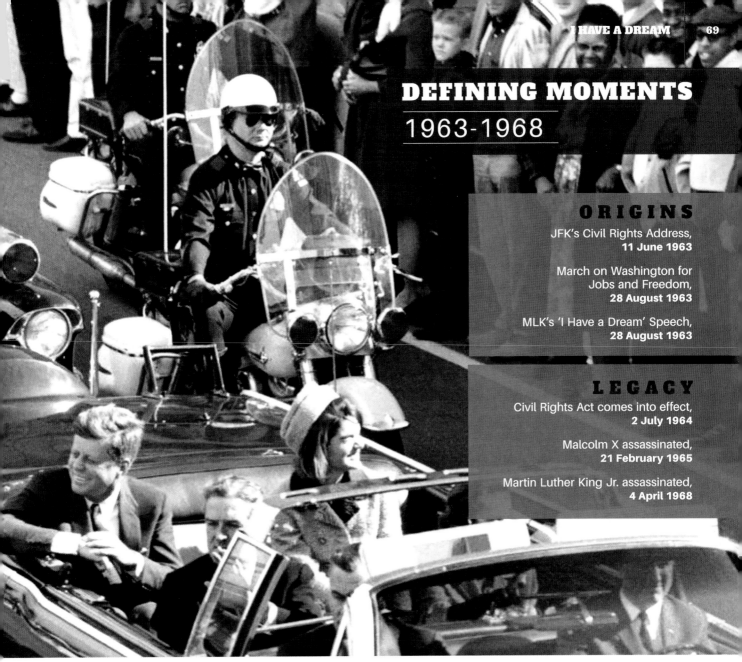

DEFINING MOMENTS
1963-1968

ORIGINS

JFK's Civil Rights Address,
11 June 1963

March on Washington for
Jobs and Freedom,
28 August 1963

MLK's 'I Have a Dream' Speech,
28 August 1963

LEGACY

Civil Rights Act comes into effect,
2 July 1964

Malcolm X assassinated,
21 February 1965

Martin Luther King Jr. assassinated,
4 April 1968

Voting Rights Act 1965

One of many legislative acts that followed in the wake of the landmark Civil Rights Act 1964, the Voting Rights Act 1965 finally put an end to racial discrimination in the American voting system. Designed to enhance and expand the principles of the 14th and 15th Amendments, this new act ensured any racial minority in the country had the legal right to cast their vote in an official ballot.

MLK's 'Mountaintop' speech in Memphis
3 April 1968

The day before he was fatally shot dead in a motel, Martin Luther King Jr. took to the stage at a rally in Memphis, Tennessee and gave one of his many memorable speeches. Now known as the 'I've Been to the Mountaintop' speech, MLK addressed the Memphis Sanitation Strike and the need for unity and cooperation.

Fair Housing Act 1968

A mere week after the shocking assassination of nonviolent civil rights leader Martin Luther King Jr., President Lyndon B. Johnson was able to pass the Fair Housing Act through Congress. Much like the Civil Rights and Voting Rights acts, this piece of legislation helped protect the sale, rental and ownership of housing for racial minorities.

"I HAVE A DREAM"

Explore the blood, sweat and tears behind one of the most iconic speeches in American history

Martin Luther King, the pastor who believed in nonviolent protest, addressed the hundreds of thousands of people gathered in Washington, DC with these words: "I am happy to join with you today in what will go down in history as the greatest demonstration for freedom in the history of our nation." The date was 28 August 1963 and while he spoke confidently, no one really knew how significant his role and the words he was yet to speak, sharing his iconic dream, would be in bringing it to life.

The day's events – known officially as The March on Washington for Jobs and Freedom – had been in planning since December 1962. An original focus on unemployment among the black population had swiftly expanded to include the broader issue of segregation and discrimination, and soon a programme of speeches, song and prayer had been arranged, reflecting a powerful vision of racial equality. Dr. Martin Luther King – the man now synonymous with the march and arguably black history itself – was last on the bill.

Proceedings started early. Word of the march had spread far and wide, and at 8am the first of 21 chartered trains arrived in the capital, followed by more than 2,000 buses and ten aeroplanes – all in addition to standard scheduled public transport. Around 1,000 people – black and white – poured into Lincoln Memorial every five minutes, including a number of well-known celebrities, which gave the march extra visibility. Charlton Heston and Burt Lancaster were among the demonstrators, as was Marlon Brando, brandishing an electric cattle prod – a less-than-subtle symbol of police brutality. Soon speakers were preparing to give their speeches to an audience of a quarter of a million, a far greater number than the 100,000 hoped for.

The growing crowd buzzed with hope and optimism, but undercurrents of unease also rippled through the throng. Against a backdrop of violent civil rights protests elsewhere around the country, President Kennedy had been reluctant to allow the march to go ahead, fearing an atmosphere of unrest. Despite the organisers' promise of

King gave his speech to just under a quarter of a million people

GANDHI'S INFLUENCE

While the two never met in person, King derived a great deal of inspiration from Mahatma Gandhi's success in nonviolent protest, and so in 1959, made the journey to Bombay (now known as Mumbai).

King and his entourage were greeted with a warm welcome: "Virtually every door was open to us", King later recorded. He noted that Indian people "love to listen to the Negro spirituals", and so his wife, Coretta, ended up singing to crowds as often as King lectured.

The trip affected King deeply. In a radio broadcast made on his last night in India, he said: "Since being in India, I am more convinced than ever before that the method of nonviolent resistance is the most potent weapon available to oppressed people in their struggle for justice and human dignity."

"King was a man who had endured death threats, bomb scares, multiple arrests and prison sentences"

a peaceful protest, the Pentagon had readied thousands of troops in the suburbs and nearly 6,000 police officers patrolled the area. Liquor sales were banned throughout the city, hospitals stockpiled blood plasma and cancelled elective surgeries, and prisoners were moved to other facilities – measures taken to prepare for the civil disobedience many thought an inevitable consequence of the largest march of its kind in US history.

Many of those attending the march feared for their own safety but turned up on that warm August day because of how important they believed it was for their country, which was being ripped apart at the seams by race. In his book, Like a Mighty Stream, Patrik Henry Bass reported that demonstrator John Marshall Kilimanjaro, who travelled to the march from Greensboro, North Carolina, said

The long road to civil rights in America

1619
- **First Known Slaves**
The first known instance of African slavery in the fledgling English Colonial America is recorded.

1712
- **New York Slave Revolt**
A group of 23 enslaved Africans kill nine white people. More than 70 blacks are arrested and 21 subsequently executed. After the uprising, the laws governing black people are made more restrictive.

1780
- **A Minor Victory**
Pennsylvania becomes the first state in the newly formed United States to abolish slavery by law.

1790-1810
- **Manumission Of Slaves**
Slaveholders in the upper South free their slaves following the revolution, and the percentage of free blacks rises from one per cent to ten per cent.

1863
- **The Emancipation Proclamation**
President Abraham Lincoln proclaims the freedom of blacks still in slavery across ten states – around 3.1 million people.

1865
- **Black Codes**
Black Codes are passed across the United States – but most notoriously in the South – restricting the freedom of black people and condemning them to low-paid labour.

that many attending the march felt afraid. "We didn't know what we would meet. There was no precedent. Sitting across from me was a black preacher with a white collar. We talked. Every now and then, people on the bus sang Oh Freedom and We Shall Overcome, but for the most part there wasn't a whole bunch of singing. We were secretly praying that nothing violent happened."

Kilimanjaro travelled over 480 kilometres (300 miles) to attend the march. Many from Birmingham, Alabama – where King was a particularly prominent figure – travelled for more than 20 hours by bus, covering 1,200 kilometres (750 miles). Attendees had invested a great deal of time, money and hope in the march, and anticipation – nervous or otherwise – was high.

The headline speaker, Martin Luther King, prominent activist, revered pastor and diligent president of the Southern Christian Leadership Conference (SCLC) had yet to finalise his speech, despite retiring to bed at 4am the previous night after a long and wearied debate with his advisors. "The logistical preparations for the march were so burdensome that the speech was not a priority for us", King's confidante and speechwriter Clarence B. Jones has since admitted.

It wasn't until the evening before the march that seven individuals, including Jones, gathered together with King to give their input on the final remarks. It was Jones's job to take notes and turn them into a powerful address that would captivate the hearts and minds of the nation – no mean feat as everyone at the meeting had a significant stake in the speech and wanted their voice to be heard. "I tried to summarise the various points made by all of his

One of the many trains from New York arrives at Washington's Union Station for the march

Clarence B. Jones, one of King's speech writers

Folk singers Joan Baez and Bob Dylan singing at the 1963 Civil Rights March on Washington

1876-1960
- **Jim Crow Laws**
  The enactment of racial segregation laws create 'separate but equal' status for African Americans, whose conditions were often inferior to those provided for white Americans.

1964
- **The Civil Rights Act**
  One of the most sweeping pieces of equality legislation seen in the US, the Civil Rights Act prohibited discrimination of any kind and gave federal government the power to enforce desegregation.

1991
- **A Stronger Act**
  President George HW Bush finally signs the Civil Rights Act of 1991, which strengthens existing civil rights law - but only after two years of debates and vetoes.

2009
- **The First Black President**
  Barack Obama is sworn in as the 44th President of the United States – the first African American in history to become the US President.

"In a heartbeat, King had done away with his formal address and began to preach from his heart and his vision"

WHAT YOU NEED TO KNOW ABOUT THE LANGUAGE OF THE SPEECH

Dr. Catherine Brown, head of faculty and senior lecturer in English at New College of the Humanities, London

• "The speech derives its power from a combination of disparate elements. On one hand, it is addressed to a particular time and place, and emphasises this fact: the situation is urgent; now is the time change must happen. On the other, the speech is dense with allusions to the Bible and foundational American documents and speeches.

• King is explicitly saying that the Emancipation Proclamation is a 'bad check' that has yet to be honoured in regard to 'the Negro people', and the speech calls on that cheque to be honoured.

• The other texts he refers to were not written by black people, but by using their phrases and rhythms he is asserting his place – and the black person's place – in the cultural, intellectual, and political tradition that they're part of. In his very words, he is not allowing himself to be 'separate but equal.'

• Behind the rhetoric of all these American texts is that of the King James translation of the Bible, and the rhetoric of ancient Greek and Roman orators. Both empires, and the authors of the Bible, are multiethnic; white supremacy would have been foreign to them."

heard. "I tried to summarise the various points made by all of his supporters", wrote Jones in his book, Behind the Dream. "It was not easy; voices from every compass point were ringing in my head." According to Jones, King soon became frustrated, telling his advisors: "I am now going upstairs to my room to counsel with my Lord. I will see you tomorrow."

No doubt the magnitude of the task at hand weighed heavily on King's mind that night as he tried to rest. By this point, King was a well-known political figure, but few outside the black church and activism circles had heard him speak publicly at length. With the relatively newfangled television networks preparing to project his image into the homes of millions, King knew that he must seize the unprecedented platform for civil rights.

When he was finally called to the podium, it was clear King's placement on the bill had put him at an immediate disadvantage. An oppressively hot day was quickly draining the crowd's enthusiasm and many had already left the march in order to make their long journeys home. A state-of-the-art sound system had been brought in for the day, but an act of sabotage before the event meant that even with help from the US Army Signal Corps in fixing it, some of the crowd struggled to hear the speakers. But King was a man who had endured death threats, bomb scares, multiple ar-

King's Speech: by the numbers

11 TIMES KING SAYS THE WORD 'DREAM'

17 MINUTES – THE LENGTH OF THE SPEECH

20 HOURS SPENT ON A BUS BY MANY TRAVELLING TO THE MARCH

100 BUSES ARRIVING PER HOUR BY 8AM

5,900 POLICE OFFICERS ON DUTY

250,000 PEOPLE AT THE MARCH

IN THE PAPERS

Newspapers around the country brandished mixed headlines following King's speech. While many reported on the march's orderly and peaceful nature, several complained of the event's effects on traffic and transport in the area. Others, perhaps deliberately, gave the march only a few column inches, referring to it as a 'racial march' rather than a call for equality.

This front page from the *Eugene Register Guard* reflects the apprehension felt by many at the time. "Massive Negro Demonstration 'Only a Beginning'" is somewhat scare mongering, implying the US should be fearful of the black population. The strapline "No Evidence of any Effect on Congress", meanwhile, seems to purposely undermine the efforts of those involved in the march.

Many of the leaders of the protest are held back before the March on Washington

equality; he would not be undone by unfortunate circumstance.

Placing his typed yet scrawl-covered notes on the lectern, King began to speak, deftly and passionately, invoking the Declaration of Independence, the Emancipation Proclamation and the US Constitution. Early on, he gave a nod toward Abraham Lincoln's Gettysburg Address ("Five score years ago..."), an equally iconic speech that, 100 years previously, set down the then-president's vision for human equality. King used rhythmic language, religious metaphor and the repetition of a phrase at the beginning of each sentence: "One hundred years later..." he cries, highlighting Lincoln's failed dream. "We cannot be satisfied..." he announces, boldly declaring that "America has given the Negro people a bad check."

Jones, watching King captivate the crowd, breathed a sigh of relief. "A pleasant shock came over me as I realised that he seemed to be essentially reciting those suggested opening paragraphs I had scrawled down the night before in my hotel room", he reveals in Behind the Dream. Then something unscripted happened. During a brief pause, gospel singer Mahalia Jackson, who had

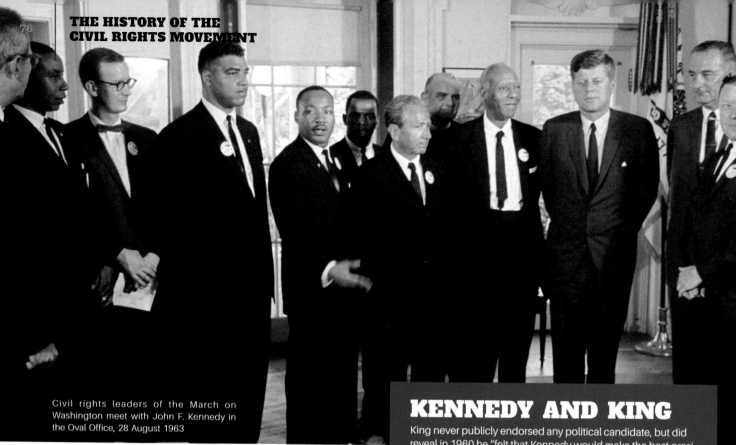

Civil rights leaders of the March on Washington meet with John F. Kennedy in the Oval Office, 28 August 1963

"King was targeted as a major enemy of the US and subjected to extensive surveillance and wiretapping by the FBI"

performed earlier in the day, shouted "Tell 'em about the dream, Martin!" King pushed his notes to one side and stood tall in front of his audience. Jones, sensing what was about to happen, told the person next to him, "These people out there today don't know it yet, but they're about to go to church."

In a heartbeat, King had done away with his formal address and began to preach from his heart his vision, his dream, which came to represent a legacy that would change civil rights forever. "I have a dream", he said, in one of the speech's most famous lines, "that my four little children will one day live in a nation where they will not be judged by the colour of their skin but by the content of their character."

"Aw, sh**", remarked Walker Wyatt, another of King's advisors. "He's using the dream." Wyatt had previously advised King to stay away from his dream rhetoric. "It's trite, it's cliché. You've used it too many times already", he warned. Indeed, King had used the refrain on several occasions before at fundraisers and rallies but, crucially, in the days before mass media it had not been publicised. To the millions watching on TV and in person, the speech was as original as they come.

When King had talked about his 'dream' before, it had been generally well received, but certainly hadn't been groundbreaking. This time, however, it was different: thousands upon thousands of listening voices cried out in approval and unity, and King's final line: "Free at last, free at last, thank God Almighty – we are free at last!" was met with a rapturous standing ovation from

KENNEDY AND KING

King never publicly endorsed any political candidate, but did reveal in 1960 he "felt that Kennedy would make the best president".

Many claim Kennedy owed his presidency to King after securing his release from prison following a protest in Atlanta, Georgia – a gesture that helped gain a large proportion of the black vote. But when the pair discussed the possibility of a second Emancipation Proclamation, Kennedy was slow to act.

Kennedy was caught between opposing forces: on one side, his belief in equality, and on the other, a preoccupation with foreign threats such as communism.

King delivers his iconic speech from the Lincoln Memorial

the enormous crowd.

King's speech was a defining moment in black history and the fight for civil rights. "Though he was extremely well known before he stepped up to the lectern," Jones wrote, "he had stepped down on the other side of history." Even President Kennedy, no

The March was attended by around 250,000 supporters

THE SPEECH'S LEGACY

Despite the success of King's speech, his address was largely forgotten afterwards, due to the speed of subsequent events, and to King's increasing disillusionment with his dream. He said that it had "turned into a nightmare." According to William P Jones, author of *The March on Washington*, in the mid-1960s "most people would not have said it was the most powerful speech ever."

King's assassination led the nation to rediscover his speech, yet remarkably the full speech did not appear in writing until 15 years later, when a transcript was published in the *Washington Post*.

The original copy of the speech is currently owned by George Raveling. The then-26-year-old basketball player had volunteered at the last minute as a bodyguard during the march, and after King's speech asked him if he could have his notes. Raveling has been offered as much as £1.8 million ($3 million) for the original copy, but he says he has no intention of selling it.

mean orator himself, reportedly turned to an aide and remarked: "He's damned good."

However, the clout of King's address was not entirely positive. The Federal Bureau of Intelligence (FBI) was wary of King's activities, and its director J. Edgar Hoover considered King to be a dangerous radical. Two days after the march, FBI agent William C. Sullivan wrote a memo about King's increasing sway: "In the light of King's powerful demagogic speech yesterday he stands head and shoulders above all other Negro leaders put together when it comes to influencing great masses of Negroes. We must mark him now, if we have not done so before, as the most dangerous Negro [...] in this nation from the standpoint of communism, the Negro and national security."

From this point on, King was targeted as a major enemy of the US and subjected to extensive surveillance and wiretapping by the FBI. According to Marshall Frady in his biography, *Martin Luther King Jr: A Life*, the FBI even sent King intercepted recordings of his extramarital affairs in a thinly veiled attempt, King believed, to intimidate and drive him to suicide.

It seems incredible to believe, but contemporary criticism not only came from the establishment, but from King's peers. Civil rights activist and author Anne Moody made the trip to Washington, DC from Mississippi for the march and recalls: "I sat on the grass and listened to the speakers, to discover we had 'dreamers' instead of leaders leading us. Just about every one of them stood up there dreaming. Martin Luther King went on and on talking about his dream. I sat there thinking that in Canton we never had time to sleep, much less dream."

Human rights activist Malcolm X also famously condemned the march, as well as Dr. King's speech itself. Allegedly dubbing the event "the farce on Washington", he later wrote in his autobiography: "Who ever heard of angry revolutionaries swinging their bare feet together with their oppressor in lily pad pools, with gospels and guitars and 'I have a dream' speeches?"

Whatever some of the critics might have said, though, there was no doubt that King's speech singled him out as a leader. His oration has been lauded as one of the greatest of the 20th century, earned him the title of 'Man of the Year' by Time Maga-

The casket of Martin Luther King Jr. was followed by more than 100,000 mourners

zine, and subsequently led to him receiving the Nobel Peace Prize. At the time, he was the youngest person to have been awarded the honour.

Most importantly, though, both the march and King's speech initiated debate and paved the way for genuine and tangible civil rights reforms, putting racial equality at the top of the agenda. The Civil Rights Act of 1964 – landmark legislation that outlawed discrimination based on race, colour, religion, sex or national origin – was enacted less than a year after King shared his dream.

Halfway through the speech, before doing away with his notes, Martin Luther King Jr. declared to his thousands of brothers and sisters in the crowd: "We cannot walk alone." That he spoke from his heart in such a poetic and unrepentant way ensured that, in the coming years, nobody did.

FOUR LITTLE GIRLS GONE

The terror bombing of the 16th Street Baptist Church in Birmingham killed four young girls and fuelled the ardour of the Civil Rights Movement

I t was a heinous act of racially motivated hatred, and an entire nation, indeed the world, recoiled in horror. How could such violence, such terror happen in the United States of America?

However, in the segregated South of the 1960s, and particularly the city of Birmingham, Alabama, white supremacist terror bombings were all too common. The state's hub of industry and commerce also became its epicentre of racial unrest when leaders of the Civil Rights Movement chose the city as a focus for their efforts to end the era of Jim Crow and segregation.

While segregation was a way of life across the South, Alabama governor George Wallace and Birmingham commissioner of public safety 'Bull' Connor were staunch adversaries of the desegregation effort. Their public denunciation of equality among the races fomented turmoil. Connor was well known for employing brutal tactics to suppress demonstrators. Images of Birmingham police officers wielding clubs, fire hoses playing on crowds, and vicious dogs straining against leashes were common fare on nightly network television news broadcasts.

Dr. Martin Luther King Jr., the acknowledged leader of the Civil Rights Movement and the nonviolent Southern Christian Leadership Conference, recognised that the increasing violence in Birmingham was the by-product of the city's racist reputation, not only due to the hostility of local government and its militantly active Ku Klux Klan (KKK) chapter, but also the fact that the desegregation effort was centred there. Demonstrations and local meetings of civil rights activists often originated at the 16th Street Baptist Church, a predominantly black congregation in the heart of the city. King himself had experienced the toxic local race relations in Birmingham in the spring of 1963, arrested there while leading nonviolent protests.

On 28 August 1963, King stood on the steps of the Lincoln Memorial in Washington, DC and delivered his stirring 'I Have a Dream' speech. Scarcely two weeks later, on 15 September, about 200 members of the 16th Street Baptist Church were attending Sunday School and preparing for later services. At 10.22am, a powerful explosion shattered the morning calm. Interior walls of the structure that had occupied the corner of 16th Street and 6th Avenue North since 1911 were demolished, shards of brick flew in every direction, stained glass windows 100 feet away were smashed, and an angry cloud billowed skyward. At least 15 sticks of dynamite had been planted on the east side of the church with a detonator set for Sunday morning, at a time when innocent people would surely be present.

Four young girls, 14-year-olds Carole Robertson, Addie Mae Collins and Cynthia Wesley, and 11-year-old Denise McNair, were killed, their battered bodies recovered from a basement restroom. Twenty-two others were injured,

So many terror bombings occurred in Birmingham that the city was often called 'Bombingham'

"At least 15 sticks of dynamite had been planted on the east side of the church, with a detonator set for Sunday morning"

Four young girls were murdered with a bomb planted by white supremacist terrorists at the 16th Street Baptist Church

The Bible lesson at the church that fateful morning was from the Gospel of Matthew, advocating love and forgiveness

The Civil Rights t of 1964 became w on 2 July that ar, months after e bombing of the church

JUSTICE DELAYED BUT DELIVERED

In the early 1970s, Alabama attorney general Bill Baxley reopened the case of the 16th Street Baptist Church bombing. The case had not grown cold due to lack of leads or evidence, but more correctly due to the indifference and outright stonewalling of the Federal Bureau of Investigation under the heavy hand of director J. Edgar Hoover, who led the FBI for decades and ordered the case closed in 1968 without action. Baxley charged Robert Edward Chambliss, also known as 'Dynamite Bob', who was convicted in 1977 and died in prison in 1985 while continuing to proclaim his innocence.

The second conviction did not occur for another 16 years. In 2001, Thomas Edwin Blanton Jr. was found guilty of murder. He remains in custody at the St Clair Correctional Facility in Springville, Alabama. In 2002, Bobby Frank Cherry, a truck driver and welder, was also sentenced to life in prison. Considering himself a "political prisoner," he died behind bars in 2004. One of Cherry's sons, one of his four ex-wives and an informant had testified against him at trial. A fourth probable conspirator, Herman Frank Cash, was never charged, although he was implicated as early as 1965. He died in 1994.

After his arrest for the 16th Street Baptist Church bombing in September 1963, Robert Edward Chambliss smiles for photographers

including 12-year-old Sarah Collins, who lost an eye. Apparently in response to a federal court order to desegregate the public schools in the state of Alabama, the blast was the third terror bombing in Birmingham in the span of 11 days.

In the wake of the tragedy, Dr. King addressed a gathering of 8,000 mourners at the funeral for three of the girls. He remarked, "These children – unoffending, innocent and beautiful – were the victims of one of the most vicious and tragic crimes ever perpetrated against humanity." A wave of violence erupted across Birmingham. Two black demonstrators were killed, and the National Guard was eventually deployed to restore order.

Although the perpetrators of the murders were probably well known, and specific individuals affiliated with the Birmingham KKK were identified, the wheels of justice turned slowly. The Federal Bureau of Investigation (FBI) gathered incriminating evidence against the suspects, but little was done under the administration of FBI director J. Edgar Hoover, an opponent of the Civil Rights Movement. After Hoover's death in 1972, the case was reopened on four separate occasions. Three of the four white supremacist suspects were convicted and sentenced to life in prison, the last of them brought to account 38 years after the incident. The fourth suspect died before he could be brought to trial.

The martyred children of the 16th Street Baptist Church did not die in vain. The bombing raised such an outcry against segregation that it surely hastened the reforms that followed in the turbulent decade of the 1960s.

Lee Harvey Oswald supported the campaign for civil rights and, according to a friend, approved of Kennedy's support of it

JFK AND MLK

How John F. Kennedy and Martin Luther King Jr. became allies of convenience, and laid the foundations for the Civil Rights Act

President John F. Kennedy and Martin Luther King Jr. shared an era and a visionary talent for inspiring Americans. Tragically, both JFK and MLK were, like Kennedy's brother Robert, assassinated before they could realise their promise as leaders. Yet Kennedy and King, the Catholic from Boston and the Baptist from Atlanta, were never particularly close either as friends or as political allies.

Kennedy and King met for the first time in June 1960. King was the leader of the black churchmen of the Southern Christian Leadership Conference (SCLC), a major civil rights organisation. His bravery in the face of intimidation and murder threats, and the eloquence and conviction of his appeals for moral justice, had made him the most prominent voice of the civil rights campaign. His enemies, the people who kept Southern blacks in second-class status, were Democrats.

Kennedy was a Democratic senator from Massachusetts, seeking to secure his party's nomination as the Democratic Party's nominee for the November 1960 presidential election. This forced Kennedy into a delicate balancing act, and not just because some of the civil rights leaders had communist or socialist pasts. In 1960, the Democratic Party was two parties. In the cities of the Northern states, the Democratic Party was the party of labour unions and ethnic minorities, including Jews, Catholics and the black workers who had migrated northwards during the Depression and World War II.

In the South, however, the Democrats remained the Democratic Party of the Civil War and Jim Crow, a racist, anti-Semitic and anti-Catholic party. In 1960, the flag of the Democratic Party in Alabama carried the words 'White Supremacy'. Many Southern Democrats were open racists, like 'Bull' Connor who, as commissioner for public safety in Birmingham, Alabama, was to direct the police to use fire hoses and attack dogs against unarmed civil rights protesters in 1963.

After meeting King, Kennedy openly praised civil rights campaigners for their "moving examples of moral courage", and called their peaceful protests "a sign of responsibility, of good citizenship, of the American spirit". When asked about the 'sit-ins', at which black customers entered whites-only restaurants and demanded to be served, Kennedy defended their ambitions and methods: "It is in the American tradition to stand up for one's rights – even if the new way to stand up for one's rights is to sit down."

To win the Democratic nomination, Kennedy needed the votes of white Southern Democrats. To win the presidency, he needed the votes of black Northern Democrats. So while Kennedy cultivated the black vote in the North by public statements, his aides urged King to suspend nonviolent protests for the remainder of 1960. King refused to compromise. Civil rights protests continued through the autumn of 1960, and the pre-election polls showed Kennedy neck-and-neck with the Republican candidate, Richard Nixon.

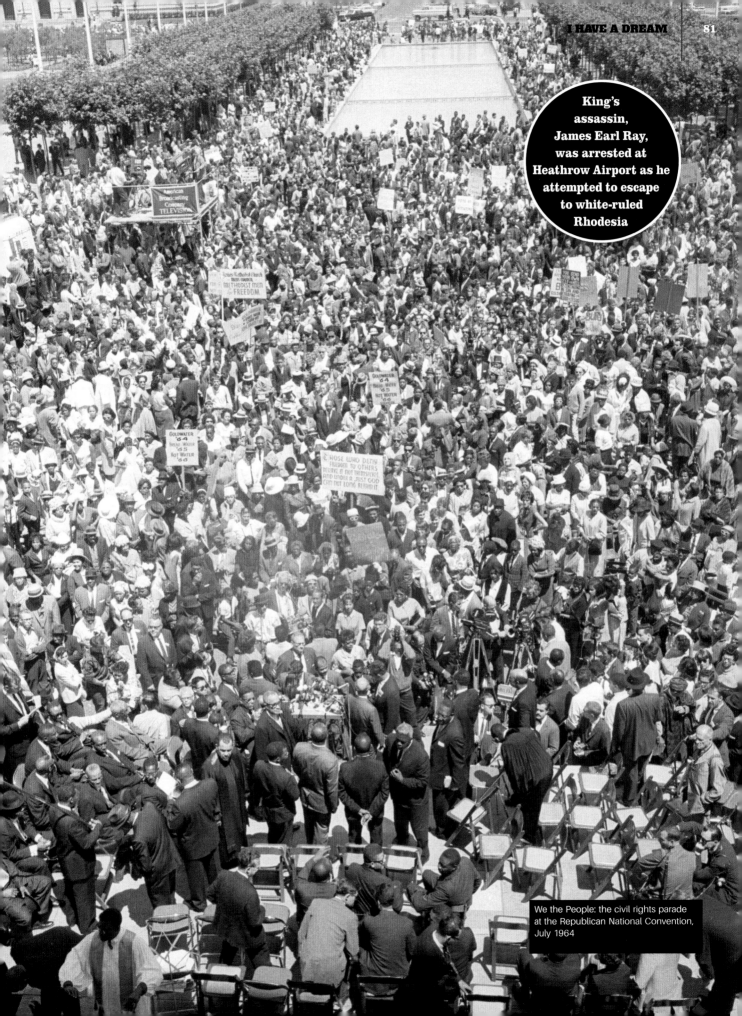

King's assassin, James Earl Ray, was arrested at Heathrow Airport as he attempted to escape to white-ruled Rhodesia

We the People: the civil rights parade at the Republican National Convention, July 1964

"Wary of splitting his party in the first months of his presidency, Kennedy avoided taking action on civil rights"

Two weeks before the election, King was arrested in a sit-in at an Atlanta department store. The police held him, alleging violation of the penalty for a prior traffic offence, and then moved him 320 kilometres (200 miles) to a maximum security state prison. As Kennedy and Nixon held their final TV debate, King began a sentence of six months' hard labour.

Kennedy chose not to speak out, but he and his brother Robert tried discreetly to secure King's release. Overruling Robert Kennedy's advice, JFK's advisers Sargent Shriver and Harris Wofford persuaded him to phone King's wife Coretta, who was six months' pregnant.

King was released on bail the next day. He thanked Kennedy for his intervention, and noted that Nixon had not helped at all.

Although King did not endorse Kennedy, news of the phone call may have helped swing the black vote in the North to Kennedy. It certainly altered the vote of King's father, Martin Luther King Sr., who had previously refused to vote for Kennedy because he was a Catholic.

Kennedy won the election, but did he manage to win Martin Luther King Jr's freedom? King appeared not to believe so. In 2014, the National Civil Rights Museum in Memphis, Tennessee, aired a reel-to-reel tape recording in which King credited the Kennedy brothers' efforts, but was somewhat reserved in his praise.

"Now, it is true that Senator Kennedy did take a specific step," King told an interviewer. "He was in contact with officials in Georgia during my arrests and he called my wife, made a personal call and expressed his concern, and said to her that he was working and trying to do something to make my release possible." Robert Kennedy, King said, had also helped. "His brother, who at that time was his campaign manager, also made direct contact with officials and even a judge in Georgia." But King did not believe that the Kennedys alone had secured his release. "So the Kennedy family did have some part in the release, but I must make it clear that many other forces worked to bring it about also."

Although John F. Kennedy believed that laws granting minorities equal access to housing and voting were inevitable, he knew that civil rights was a partisan issue – in his own party as much as in the country at large. He believed other issues were more pressing: taxes, steel prices, Fidel Castro's hostile government in Cuba, and the pursuit of the Cold War. He wanted to secure the support of liberal Republicans for civil rights legislation. That meant backroom negotiations.

Wary of splitting his party in the first months of his presidency, Kennedy avoided taking action on civil rights. Although King was the most prominent civil rights leader, he was not invited to Kennedy's inauguration, or to Kennedy's sop to civil rights, a first meeting at the White House with civil rights leaders. The Kennedys wanted to control the pace of civil rights, so that it did not upset the broader strategy of JFK's first term, including the key element of any president's first-term strategy; the winning of a second term.

Soon, King concluded that the civil rights campaign must force Kennedy to act. As the Freedom Riders spread across the South, they encountered physical danger and hostile policing. In May 1961, King went to Montgomery, Alabama to preach in support of the Freedom Riders at

J. Edgar Hoover, chief of the FBI, in his office, September 1961

THE FBI AND MLK

The FBI spied on Martin Luther King Jr. from 1957 until his murder in 1968. The antagonism between J. Edgar Hoover and King was personal. Hoover made sure that the Kennedy brothers knew about King's adultery and the communist background of some of his associates. After the assassination of JFK in November 1963, Hoover heard recordings of King calling him "senile", and discussed with aides whether they could pressure JFK's successor Lyndon Johnson to fire Hoover. The FBI also obtained recordings of King in the act of committing adultery in hotel rooms around the country. Hoover gave copies of the tapes to President Johnson, and ordered aides to leak the story of King's sexual adventures to the press. One of Hoover's aides even mailed an audio tape of King having sex to King's wife, Coretta. A year later, when King won the Nobel Peace Prize, Hoover was to call King "the most notorious liar in the country".

King responded by asking to meet Hoover. When they met at FBI headquarters, Hoover boasted of the FBI's work against the Ku Klux Klan; the surveillance went unmentioned.

While King was in Hoover's office, an FBI man showed waiting journalists a photograph of King leaving an hotel with an unidentified woman.

During the Birmingham, Alabama campaign of 1963, King stayed at the Gaston Motel. It was bombed in May 1963

Vice President Lyndon B. Johnson takes the oath of office on Air Force One after the assassination of President Kennedy, 22 November 1963

the church of fellow SCLC leader Ralph Abernathy. Robert Kennedy, now attorney general, personally ordered the deployment of federal marshals to protect King.

King and the civil rights leaders, however, still believed that the Kennedys were not pressing civil rights with the urgency it deserved. In a speech in July 1962, King said that Kennedy should use "moral persuasion, by occasionally speaking out against segregation". Kennedy replied that his commitment to the equality of all Americans was clear. But another year passed before he would demonstrate that commitment by legislative proposals. When he did, it was because the civil rights campaign had forced the American people to become spectators of a moral crisis. The spectacle of protestors being attacked with clubs, dogs and water hoses in Alabama, and black children killed in terrorist attacks on churches, caused widespread public revulsion.

Kennedy was compelled to acknowledge that "repressive police action" and "token moves" were not the answer. In June 1963, he finally proposed legislation against Jim Crow laws in the South. All Americans with a grade-school education (up to the age of 16), would be allowed to vote. There would be no discrimination in public places like hotels and restaura nts.

Despite initiating these watershed proposals, the Kennedys kept their distance from King. They knew that the most powerful man in the government bureaucracy, J. Edgar Hoover of the FBI, loathed King and the Civil Rights Movement. They also knew that Hoover had used four decades of warrantless surveillance to amass secret files not just on the private lives of organised crime bosses and more than 400,000 suspected political

'subversives', but also on every American in public life, from Hollywood to Washington to the SCLC. That included the Kennedy brothers and Martin Luther King Jr.

Apart from an obsessive interest in his suspects' political associations, Hoover had a particular interest in sexual gossip. A political past could be disavowed, but a sexual past was less easy to escape. Hoover's investigations into the political lives of John F. Kennedy and Martin Luther King had generated material on the secret sex lives of both men, and with Robert Kennedy's knowledge.

Hoover had wiretaps showing Mafia donations to John F. Kennedy's 1960 campaign for the Democratic nomination in West Virginia, apparently disbursed by Frank Sinatra. Hoover had heard the rumour that JFK's father, Joseph Kennedy, had secured the help of Chicago mob boss Sam Giancana to stuff ballot boxes in Cook County, Illinois, a state crucial to Kennedy's narrow victory in the 1960 election. He also had evidence of links between Judith Exner, one of JFK's mistresses, and the Chicago Mafia.

As attorney general, Robert Kennedy was committed to a drive against the Mafia. FBI surveillance of the Chicago mob boss Sam Giancana led agents to Judith Exner. She turned out to be one of John F. Kennedy's lovers; later, she claimed to have acted as a go-between in the president's dealings with Giancana. In March 1962, Hoover presented JFK with evidence of Exner's ties to Sam Giancana and his Los Angeles lieutenant, John Roselli, and that her telephone records showed that she had called JFK's secretary at the White House on numerous occasions. JFK would go on to end his relationship with Exner soon after this.

Meanwhile, the FBI had been tracking Martin Luther King Jr. and the SCLC since 1957. Hoover disliked black people in general. In private, he called King "the burrhead". He was opposed to civil rights as a form of disorder and radicalism, and detected signs of organised communist conspiracy in the campaign for equal rights. The FBI investigation deepened in 1962, focusing on King's aide Hunter Pitts O'Dell, who had been a member of the Communist Party in the 1950s; his lawyer Stanley Levison, whom the FBI considered to have been a major funder of the Communist Party USA in the 1950s; and Bayard Rustin, who had introduced King to Levison, and who, apart from a communist past, also had convictions for homosexual activity.

When Kennedy received King at the White House in June 1963, he told him that the FBI was bugging him. At the same time, Kennedy publicly disapproved of the March on Washington, planned for 28 August 1963. "We want success in the Congress, not a big show on the Capitol," he explained. When A Philip Randolph, the head of the March on Washington, asked Kennedy to lead a "crusade" for civil rights, Kennedy explained that he preferred to work for legislative progress in a bipartisan deal with liberal Republicans. Kennedy also had to neutralise J. Edgar Hoover. The White House recruited white union groups to the march, to pre-empt claims that civil rights was an issue for black radicals.

On 22 November 1963, Kennedy was assassinated in Dallas, Texas.

"His death is a great loss to America and the world," commented Martin Luther King Jr. "The finest tribute that the American people can pay to the late President Kennedy is to implement the progressive policies that he sought to initiate in foreign and domestic policies." Kennedy's vice president, Lyndon Johnson, took over, and won the 1964 election. Unlike Kennedy, Johnson had a deep commitment to civil rights. He was determined to push through legislation, regardless of the cost to the Democratic Party. The result was the bipartisan Civil Rights Act (1964) and Voting Rights Act (1965).

"We have lost the South for a generation," Johnson is reported to have said after signing the Civil Rights Act. Johnson was prepared to pay that price. Historians continue to argue over whether JFK would have risked his party's unity and the presidency over civil rights, an issue that ranked low among his priorities, and on which he only acted due to public pressure.

While Johnson worked for the Civil Rights Act, Robert Kennedy permitted Hoover's surveillance of King. It appears that when Robert Kennedy collaborated with Hoover against the Mafia, he had no idea about his brother's links to Exner and Giancana. Robert Kennedy did, however, know about Hoover's surveillance of Martin Luther King Jr. In December 1963, just weeks after the killing of JFK, Hoover secured Robert Kennedy's permission to bug King's hotel rooms and tap his phones. The

Civil rights leaders (from left): Martin Luther King Jr., Attorney General Robert Kennedy, Roy Wilkins and Vice President Lyndon Johnson

pretext was that King's lawyer, Stanley Levison, had previously been a member of the Communist Party. Hoover's real objective was to destroy King and the civil rights campaign. Although Kennedy had authorised the surveillance on "a trial basis, for a month or so", it actually continued until King's murder in April 1968.

Although King criticised him and the Department of Justice for not prosecuting civil rights violations during JFK's presidency, King thanked Robert Kennedy for his work in securing the passage of the Civil Rights Act: "Your able, courageous and effective work in guiding the Civil Rights Act of 1964 through both Houses of Congress has earned for you an even warmer spot in the hearts of freedom-loving people the world over. I add to theirs my sincere and heartfelt thanks."

In September 1964, Robert Kennedy stepped down from the attorney generalship. Two months later, Kennedy won a senate race for New York, and began to position himself for the campaign for the 1968 Democratic Party nomination. In 1966, when Kennedy criticised Johnson's involvement in Vietnam, King congratulated him. A year later, King gave a detailed anti-Vietnam speech. The two seemed likely to represent the future of America, domestically and internationally. Instead, they came to represent its tragedy.

On 4 April 1968, a white racist named James Earl Ray shot King in the head as he stood on the balcony of a motel in Memphis, Tennessee. As riots broke out in major cities across America, Robert Kennedy pleaded with a mostly black audience in downtown Indianapolis, Indiana to follow King's ideals of nonviolence.

Over the following weeks, Kennedy surged towards the Democratic nomination. On 6 June 1968, Kennedy, having delivered a speech at a hotel in Los Angeles, was shot and killed. His assassin, a Palestinian immigrant named Sirhan Sirhan, cited American support for Israel as the motive for Kennedy's killing.

Richard Milhous Nixon, 37th President of the United States of America, and beneficiary of the Southern Strategy

The triple assassinations of JFK, MLK and RFK profoundly damaged American society, pushing American politics onto a different track. Richard Nixon, who had narrowly lost the 1960 election to JFK, won the 1968 election with a promise to extricate America from Vietnam, and restore order at home.

RACE RESHAPES AMERICAN POLITICS

In the 1960 election, JFK won 78 per cent of the black vote. Martin Luther King voted for Kennedy, though he did not endorse Kennedy or admit it at the time. "Had President Kennedy lived," King wrote after Kennedy's assassination, "I would probably have endorsed him in 1964." Instead, King called on "all people of goodwill" to not vote Republican in the 1964 election.

The Democratic Party remains the most popular choice among black voters. But civil rights legislation caused the transformation of the Southern white vote. In 1960, JFK had also carried the majority of the white Southern vote. In 1964, some Southern Democrats supported Republican candidate Barry Goldwater. The passage of the Civil Rights Act later that year precipitated the collapse of support for the Democratic Party among white Southerners. In 1968, Richard Nixon and the Republicans carried the Southern white vote. Nixon's chief of staff, H.R. Haldeman, advised a strategy that insinuated that "the whole problem is really the blacks", while ostensibly speaking about "law and order".

The redrawing of affiliations in the wake of civil rights legislation reshaped American politics to this day. The Democratic Party has shaken off its historic associations with slavery and Jim Crow, while the Republican Party struggles to shake off the taint of the 'Southern Strategy'.

In 1975, Nixon's chief of staff H.R. Haldeman was convicted for his part in the Watergate Affair

Edgar Ray Killen, mastermind of the KKK plot to murder Schwerner, Goodman, and Chaney, was a Baptist minister

Dr. Martin Luther King Jr., holds a photograph of the three civil rights workers murdered in the summer of 1964

RACISM AND MURDER IN
MISSISSIPPI

The murders of three civil rights workers in Mississippi gained national attention, though true justice may never have been served

dgar Ray 'Preacher' Killen met his death just before his 93rd birthday sat behind bars at the state penitentiary in Parchman, convicted in the deaths of three civil rights workers in rural Mississippi in the summer of 1964. Killen's conviction as the mastermind of the murder conspiracy came in 2005, a full 41 years after the killings, not for murder but three counts of manslaughter, a lesser charge.

Justice, some say, has only been partially served to this day. The case is now closed after numerous reviews and charges against more than 20 individuals resulted in seven federal convictions for violations of the victims' human rights. The state of Mississippi would not initially indict the conspirators for murder, a state charge, and with evidence collected by the Federal Bureau of Investigation (FBI), the verdicts were obtained in jury trials after the government in Washington invoked a 19th-century statute dating back to the era of post-Civil War reconstruction.

The summer of 1964 was pivotal in the progress of the Civil Rights Movement, particularly in the South. As the Council of Federated Organizations (COFO) and its affiliate, the Congress of Racial Equality (CORE), sent volunteers to Southern states, a concerted effort was underway to register black voters. In Mississippi, white supremacists warned against

a tidal wave of civil rights workers descending upon the state during their 'Freedom Summer' campaign.

Into this smouldering cauldron, 24-year-old Michael Schwerner, a civil rights worker from New York, arrived in Meridian, Mississippi, in January 1964. On 21 June, Schwerner returned from a training programme in Ohio with 20-year-old Andrew Goodman, a new CORE volunteer from New York, and James Chaney, 21, a black worker from Mississippi. Earlier in the month, two dozen Klansmen had descended on the Mount Zion Methodist Church in Neshoba County, beaten several people, and burned the building to the ground. They had been looking for Schwerner, who was planning to establish a 'Freedom School' at the church, the plan being to organise, educate and mobilise blacks.

On 21 June, the three civil rights workers drove to the Zion Church site to investigate the terror attack. On their way back to Meridian, Neshoba County Sheriff's Deputy Cecil Price spotted their station wagon, a known CORE vehicle, travelling near the town of Philadelphia. Price pulled the car over, arrested Chaney for speeding, and also handcuffed Goodman and Schwerner on a trumped up charge of possible collusion in the church burning. Late in the afternoon, the men were jailed in Philadelphia.

Requests to make phone calls were denied, and the three spent seven

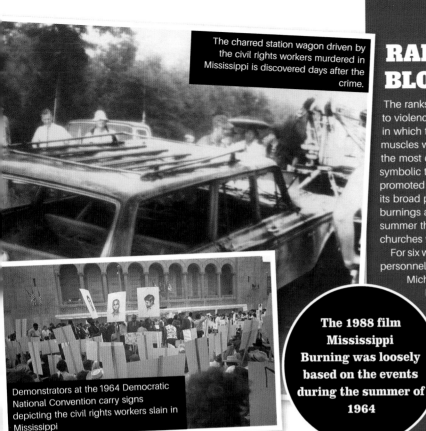

The charred station wagon driven by the civil rights workers murdered in Mississippi is discovered days after the crime.

Demonstrators at the 1964 Democratic National Convention carry signs depicting the civil rights workers slain in Mississippi

The 1988 film Mississippi Burning was loosely based on the events during the summer of 1964

RAMPAGE OF BLOOD AND TERROR

The ranks of the Mississippi Ku Klux Klan, a vile hate group prone to violence, swelled to nearly 10,000 members by 1964, a year in which the shadowy white supremacist organisation flexed its muscles with a campaign of intimidation and murder. Among the most common KKK tactics was the burning of a cross, a symbolic threat to those who were targeted, opposed the group, or promoted racial equality. On 24 April 1964, the Klan demonstrated its broad power base in Mississippi, holding simultaneous cross burnings at 61 locations across the state. During the violent summer that followed, the burnings of 20 predominantly black churches were linked to the KKK.

For six weeks, FBI agents and others, including 400 US Navy personnel from a nearby naval air station, looked for the bodies of Michael Schwerner, Andrew Goodman and James Chaney. In July, the search of the rivers, swamps, fields, and thickets yielded the bodies of eight black men. One was recovered wearing a CORE t-shirt, and was obviously a victim of murder. Two others were identified as college students Charles Moore and Henry Dee, who had been abducted, severely beaten, and executed sometime in May. Another was identified as 14-year-old Herbert Oarsby. Little information about the other four corpses was ever disclosed.

The Klansmen themselves were warned that breaking their code of silence meant death, and compounding the difficulties encountered during the investigation was the simple fact that a number of the actual perpetrators and other members of the Klan held positions of authority in Neshoba County and throughout the area.

At the height of the investigation into the murders, 200 FBI agents, many from New Orleans, were on the case

hours in jail supposedly waiting for a justice of the peace to handle the speeding fine. Around 10pm, Price allowed them to leave without coming before a court official. A member of the local KKK, Price had alerted other conspirators that the men were in custody. He followed them out of town and then returned to Philadelphia to drop off another police officer before again turning in pursuit. Price caught up with the men near the Neshoba County line and after two more vehicles stopped at the scene, Price loaded the three men in his patrol car. The three cars proceeded to a dirt lane called Rock Cut Road and stopped. Schwerner and Goodman were summarily shot in the heart. Chaney was beaten and then shot three times.

The CORE vehicle was set on fire along an abandoned logging road. It was found on 23 June during an exhaustive search for the missing men. The bodies were transported to a nearby farm and buried within a large earthen dam. After 44 days, FBI agents acting on a tip from an informant finally located them.

A series of indictments followed and in the 1967 trial, Price, Travis Barnette, Alton Roberts, Billy Wayne Posey, James Arledge, James Snowden, and Samuel Bowers were convicted of violating the slain trio's civil rights. Sentences ranged from three to ten years; however, none of them served longer than six years in prison. Eight defendants were acquitted, and three cases resulted in a hung jury. Killen remained free for decades. In further insult to the victims, no one was ever charged with murder.

Sometimes referred to as the 'Mississippi Burning' or 'Freedom Summer' murders, these needless and tragic deaths of three young men in June 1964 advanced the cause of civil rights, influencing the passage of the landmark Voting Rights Act of 1965.

"In further insult to the victims, no one was ever charged with murder"

Investigators uncover the remains of civil rights volunteers Schwerner, Goodman and Chaney under thick red clay of an earthen dam

THE LONG MARCH TO VOTE

While the Civil Rights Act had outlawed discrimination, in the South many black people were still effectively disenfranchised. In 1964, the struggle turned to the right to vote

Participants in the Selma to Montgomery marches in 1965

On the last day, marchers move along Dexter Avenue to the State Capitol building

Civil rights marchers in front of the State Capitol building at the end of their march from Selma to Montgomery

O n 2 July 1964, President Lyndon Johnson had signed the Civil Rights Act, outlawing discrimination on the basis of colour, race, religion or sex. But while the passage of the act through Congress and the Senate was a historic achievement, blacks in Southern states still faced entrenched discrimination, in particular with respect to voting rights. For instance, the Alabama state legislature required people registering to vote to pass a literacy test and pay a poll tax. What made the discrimination even more invidious was the test being administered by white people whose judgement was final and often arbitrary. Every effort was made to make it difficult for black people to even attempt to register, with restricted opening hours for centres of registration (often only one or two days a month), intimidation and threats of sacking to anyone who did try to register to vote. The end result was that in Dallas County, Alabama, according to a 1961 report, only 130 blacks were registered to vote, out of a population of 15,000 eligible voters. Dallas County, with Selma as its county seat, had a majority of black citizens but, because so many were disenfranchised, political power there lay in the hands of the white minority – and they intended to keep it.

Local activists in Selma and Dallas County had made repeated attempts to register voters but when these failed, eight people invited the Southern Christian Leadership Conference (SCLC) to assist in gaining local black people their rights. One of the factors that led the SCLC board, including Dr. Martin Luther King, to accept the invitation was the reputation the Dallas County police force, under its sheriff, Jim Clark, had for brutality. Clark employed 200 deputies, some of whom were members of the Ku Klux Klan, arming them with electric cattle prods. Dr. King and the SCLC had learned that time-honoured rule of the news media: if it bleeds, it leads. To garner the national attention they needed in order to put pressure on President Lyndon Johnson to bring forward legislation against the sort of discrimination black voters faced in places like Selma, they needed to find city authorities that were brutal enough and stupid enough to attack and beat nonviolent protestors under the lenses of TV cameramen. In Sheriff Jim Clark, King and the SCLC had found their man.

As the first stage in the campaign, Dr. King, the SCLC and local activists organised mass voter registrations to highlight the invidious restrictions placed on black voters. Unable to suppress their violent bigotry, Sheriff Clark and his men responded brutally and over 3,000 people were arrested through January 1965, including Dr. King. But despite a court ruling in favour of the civil rights protestors, by February Dr. King could still say, in a letter to the New York Times, "This is Selma, Alabama. There are more Negroes in jail

Civil rights marches cross the
Edmund Pettus Bridge in Selma,
Alabama

The marchers took great strength from the support of various religious traditions

"We March with Selma!": Protestors in New York carry banners in support of the Selma to Montgomery marchers

with me than there are on the voting rolls."

Then, on 18 February 1965, police broke up a protest in neighbouring Perry County. Trying to escape the Alabama state police, Jimmie Lee Jackson, a poor farm worker who was also a deacon in his church, took refuge in a café but the police followed him in and then shot him. Jackson managed to stagger out, but died eight days later from his wounds.

Jackson's death stoked emotions that were already running high. In order to stop the protests turning violent, SCLC organiser James Bevel proposed a march from Selma, the county seat, to Montgomery, the state capital, a distance of 80 kilometres (50 miles), to present their grievances to the governor. Dr. King was in Atlanta, so the march was led by the Reverend Hosea Williams along with student activist, John Lewis.

On Sunday 7 March, about 600 marchers set out from Selma and came to the Edmund Pettus Bridge over the Alabama River. The bridge has a central hump, so it was only when they crested the hump that the marchers realised that the police and state troopers were waiting for them on the other side. The governor of Alabama, George Wallace, had ordered that the march was to be prevented from reaching Montgomery by any means necessary: Sheriff Jim Clark needed no further encouragement. With his mounted posse, Clark charged into the marchers, beating them with clubs while police fired tear gas. Even when the protestors tried to retreat, the mounted police charged after them, still flailing with their clubs.

That evening, ABC, one of the national networks, stopped its programming to show viewers film of the brutality visited, by American

lawmen, upon nonviolent protestors. The following day, the national press was covered with pictures of police beating women and men. Sheriff Jim Clark, too stupid to stop himself or his men, had fallen for the trap that had been set for him.

In response to the violence, Dr. King called on local religious leaders to join him in a second march from Selma to Montgomery that would take place two days later, on Tuesday 9 March. But when Judge Frank Minis Johnson placed a temporary restraining order on the march, Dr. King and the other protest leaders were faced with a dilemma. Judge Johnson had given many rulings in favour of black civil rights and it was thought that he would lift the order. In the end, Dr. King led some 2,000 marchers to Edmund Pettus Bridge where they knelt and prayed, in sight of Alabama state troopers, before turning round and returning to Selma. As a result, the day became known as 'Turnaround Tuesday'.

But the protestors' nonviolence was again met by violence – that evening James Reeb, a white Unitarian Universalist minister who had joined in the march, was set on by segregationists and beaten badly. He died two days later from his injuries.

On 15 March, President Lyndon Johnson addressed a joint session of Congress, and the whole nation via television, saying, "Their cause must be our cause too. Because it is not just Negroes, but really it is all of us, who must overcome the crippling legacy of bigotry and injustice. And we shall overcome." Two days later, the president brought new legislation to ensure voting rights for black people before Congress. Meanwhile, Judge Johnson

Defining moment
Freedom Day
7 Oct 1963

Around 400 black people arrive at Dallas County Courthouse to register to vote. Annie Lee Cooper is one of the people waiting in line. The registrars work as slowly as possible and take a very long lunch break. But Freedom Day marks the beginning of the struggle for the vote in Dallas County, and Alabama more generally.

Dr. King arrested
Leading a protest, Dr. Martin Luther King is arrested and put into Selma jail.
1 February 1965

Political progress
President Lyndon Johnson says he will urge legislation for voting rights to be considered by Congress.
6 February 1965

Timeline

1963 1965

Start of the campaign
Dr. King begins the campaign. Some 700 black people come to a meeting at Brown Chapel despite a court injunction forbidding such gatherings.
2 January 1965

First attempts to register
Dr. King leads 300 marchers to the courthouse to attempt to register for the vote. Nobody manages to register.
18 January 1965

Further attempts to register
This time, when people come to try to register, Sheriff Clark arrests them.
19 January 1965

Punching back
Annie Lee Cooper, waiting to register, slugs Sheriff Clark when he pokes her with his club. She is arrested.
25 January 1965

Death in the café
Jimmie Lee Jackson, hiding from state troopers in a café, is shot in the stomach He dies eight days later.
18 February 1965

Demonstrators lock arms in front of the Dallas County courthouse in Selma, Alabama. Sheriff Jim Clark had them all arrested

THE WOMAN WHO DID NOT TURN THE OTHER CHEEK

Based as it was in Christianity, the Civil Rights Movement enjoined its activists to practise nonviolence, to turn the other cheek as Jesus had told his disciples, and the movement's followers kept to this precept with astonishing self-discipline and courage. However, under the sorts of provocation people faced, tempers could snap, and no one's temper snapped more famously than that of Annie Lee Cooper. A Selma native, she had moved when young to Kentucky, before returning to Selma in 1962 to look after her mother. Cooper had registered to vote when she lived in Kentucky and Ohio, and she was determined to vote in Alabama too, but first she had to register. She tried often, to no avail. "Once," she said, "I stood in line from 7am to 4pm but never got to register." On 7 October 1963, activists organised a Freedom Day when 400 black people, the maximum allowed by the courts, waited outside Dallas County courthouse to register, and Annie Lee Cooper stood among them. She wasn't able to register, but when her employers saw her there, they fired her. On 25 January 1965, Annie Lee Cooper tried again, joining the queue of black people waiting outside Dallas County courthouse to register to vote. But this time, Sheriff Jim Clark turned up with his deputies. Clark ordered Cooper to leave, prodding her in the neck with his club, until Annie Lee Cooper finally let go of the principles of non-violence, swung round and landed a sweet right hook on Clark's jaw, knocking him to the ground. Clark's deputies then waded in, pushing Cooper down and holding her there while the enraged Jim Clark beat her with his club. Annie Lee Cooper was arrested and held for 11 hours in jail: she sang spirituals during her imprisonment.

Cooper was played by Oprah Winfrey in the movie *Selma*

had lifted the restraining order against the marchers while also directing local law enforcement that they were not to harass the marchers.

On 21 March, the third march to Montgomery left Selma, protected by FBI agents. Among the marchers were Joe Young, a blind man from Georgia, and Jim Letherer from Michigan, who did the march on crutches. The marchers took four days to reach the state capital and the weather was often foul, but by the time they reached Montgomery the number of marchers had grown to 25,000. On their last night, as the marchers camped in the grounds of St Jude, a Catholic establishment on the outskirts of Montgomery, entertainers such as Harry Belafonte and Nina Simone performed for the excited crowd. On the morrow, they knew they would be making history.

On 25 March, Dr. King led the marchers through Montgomery. In response to reports of snipers waiting to shoot him, 15 black clergymen who looked like King walked abreast of him at the front of the procession. However, when the marchers reached the State Capitol building, Governor Wallace refused to see them. Dr. King proceeded to address the marchers and, via television, the nation.

"Our aim must never be to defeat or humiliate the white man, but to win his friendship and understanding. We must come to see that the end we seek is a society at peace with itself, a society that can live with its conscience. And that will be a day not of the white man, not of the black man. That will be the day of man as man."

Less than six months later, on 6 August 1965, President Johnson signed the Voting Rights Act, with Dr. King and other civil rights leaders by his side.

Defining moment
Bloody Sunday
7 March 1965
Not knowing what's waiting for them on the other side of Edmund Pettus Bridge, 600 marchers cross the Alabama River only to come face-to-face with Sheriff Jim Clark (left) and his deputies, mounted on horses, ready and spoiling for a fight. The police and state troopers attack the marchers, putting 16 in hospital and injuring at least 50 others. Pictures dominate the TV channels and newspapers.

Defining moment
March to Montgomery
25 March 1965
The third march from Selma to Montgomery finally reaches the intended destination and does so without injury or violence. Outside the State Capitol, Dr. Martin Luther King Jr. asks, rhetorically, how long black people will have to wait for their right to vote. The answer: "Not long, because the arc of the moral universe is long, but it bends toward justice."

● **Court orders**
The day after Bloody Sunday, Judge Frank Johnson, concerned for their safety, places a temporary injunction against further marches.
8 March 1965

● **Turnaround Tuesday**
Dr. King leads marchers to Edmund Pettus Bridge, prays there, then leads them back to Selma.
9 March 1965

● **Death of the minister**
James Reeb, with three other ministers, is attacked by the Ku Klux Klan. Reeb dies from his injuries two days later. He was 38.
11 March 1965

● **On the road again**
Marchers set out for the third time from Selma, heading to Montgomery, the state capital.
21 March 1965

● **Death in the night**
Viola Liuzzo, a white Unitarian Universalist minister and mother of five who had come to Montgomery to help with the march, was shot by the Ku Klux Klan in her car.
25 March 1965

Civil rights protesters during the second march from Selma to Montgomery encounter a police blockade. Protesters eventually turned around due to fears for public safety, leading it to be labelled Turnaround Tuesday.

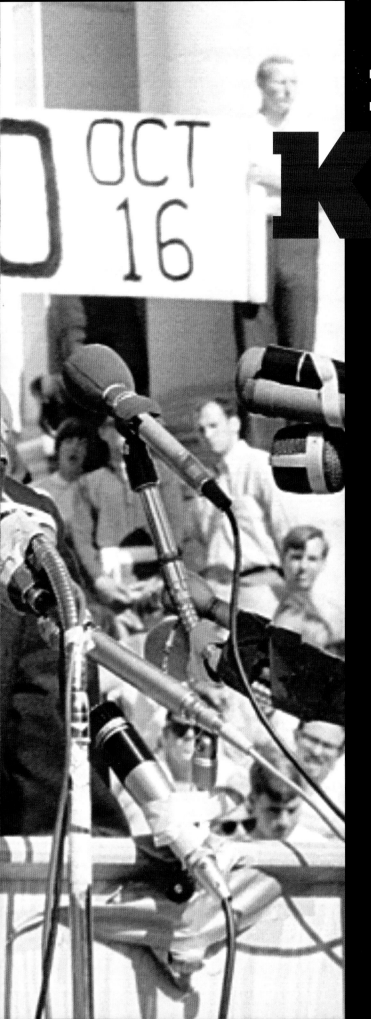

DEATH OF A
KING

Martin Luther King Jr. rose from a simple Baptist minister to a crusader for nonviolent protest and racial equality, and his death resonated around the world

The Civil Rights Movement of the 1960s – a social and political upheaval that changed the United States, and indeed the wider world – has immortalised many of its most famous activists. Some were radicals, urging African Americans to break the shackles of enforced segregation and create a new nation of black supremacy, while others preached a policy of peace, believing only diplomacy and reason could undo the prejudices of old.

Martin Luther King Jr., the son of a Baptist minister and one of the figureheads of the Civil Rights Movement throughout the 1950s and 1960s, was one such peaceful individual – but unlike his contemporaries, his legacy owes itself as much to the aftermath of his death as it does the inspirational actions of his life. As a figure campaigning for change in a country struggling to shake off its divisionist traditions, King refused to accept the segregation that forced African Americans into lives as second-class citizens.

He organised sit-ins and led rallies and protests, but always promoted a mantra of nonviolence – his position as a minister and his natural talent for public speaking made him a force of nature, captivating the media and befuddling both the radical black activists of the movement and the white traditionalists refusing to alter the status quo. It also made him a target. His life was filled with attacks and assassination attempts, but whether by luck or the grace of God, King survived almost every one.

In life, King was the voice of a new era, one that wanted to make all citizens equal in the eyes of god and the Constitution, a peaceful force in a nation ready to blow like a powder keg. In his later years, he was a key influence on the ratification of the Civil Rights Bill, which granted civil equality for African Americans, but his death helped secure the last – and perhaps the most vital – legislative change of the Civil Rights Movement: the Housing Act. The wave of mourning felt across the nation following his murder, however tragic, was exactly what was needed to ensure every citizen – regardless of colour or creed – could have a home that was protected from discrimination.

The rise to fame

15 January 1929
Born Michael King Jr. in Atlanta, Georgia, he's the middle child of Reverend Michael King and Alberta Williams King.

1934
King Sr. finds inspiration in the works of German theologian Martin Luther. He renames himself and his eldest son in tribute.

1948
King graduates with a BA in Sociology. He becomes a minister and enters the Crozer Theological Seminary in Pennsylvania.

1944
A gifted student, King graduates at the age of 15 and passes the entry exam for the prestigious Morehouse College.

1 December 1955
King joins the Montgomery Bus Boycott following Rosa Parks' arrest. Four days later, he's elected the spokesman for the movement.

1957
The Southern Christian Leadership Conference is formed by King to battle segregation and attain civil rights for African Americans.

1960
King is arrested and sentenced to four months in prison. Presidential candidate Kennedy helps to remove the sentence.

20 September 1958
While at a book signing, King is stabbed in the chest by a mentally ill woman. He is hospitalised but will make a full recovery.

13 April 1963
King launches the Birmingham campaign. Nonviolent protesters are blasted with water cannons and arrested during sit-ins.

10 May 1963
After a month of protests, the Birmingham agreement is struck, enabling African Americans to use shops and public services.

3 January 1964
After years as the figurehead of nonviolent and, more importantly, successful protests, King appears on the cover of Time magazine.

28 August 1963
King delivers his iconic 'I Have A Dream' speech to 250,000 activists on the steps of the Lincoln Memorial, Washington, DC.

2 July 1964
The Civil Rights Act is signed into law by President Lyndon B. Johnson. King and fellow activists celebrate, but many white citizens choose to ignore the new law.

4 April 1968
A day after he delivers his final 'I've Been To The Mountaintop' speech, King is fatally shot in Memphis. Riots and mourning engulf the US.

President Lyndon B. Johnson meets with Martin Luther King and other prominent civil rights activists Whitney Young and James Farmer

It's a common misconception that King and Malcolm X were close – in fact they only met once. Despite his early extreme views, Malcolm X would eventually share the same ideals of nonviolence

Martin Luther King Jr. and other civil rights activists gather to witness President Lyndon B. Johnson sign the Voting Rights Act into law

THE DAYS BEFORE

As Martin Luther King Jr. made the fateful steps towards that final evening in Memphis, the years-long Civil Rights Movement was reaching its crescendo

In 1968, after more than a decade of activism, true change was finally about to become a reality for African Americans living in the United States. Despite the abolition of slavery during the presidency of Abraham Lincoln, non-white citizens still lived a half life, forced into segregation and robbed of the equality championed in the Constitution. Now, with spring in full swing, Martin Luther King Jr. and the Civil Rights Movement had done (to some) the unthinkable: they had changed the opinions of the people with power, people with the power to change the law.

Yet with the bill mere months away from being signed into law, those final days of King's life were becoming a tense affair. The movement was splintering, with more aggressive elements, such as the Black Panthers group, bringing negative attention to the cause. Progress was being made, but riots were becoming as common as the peaceful protests that were being promoted by King. Events were boiling to a crescendo.

Of course, such a radical change did not occur overnight, but recent actions had set events into an even swifter motion. The Civil Rights bill itself had originally been called for by President John F. Kennedy in 1963 – charismatic yet ferocious in his political demeanour, JFK was a force to be reckoned with, but even he encountered considerable resistance (and calls for a counter bill) in the Senate. His assassination later that year rocked the nation, but it also passed the presidency to Lyndon B. Johnson – a man as passionate about achieving true equality for American citizens as his predecessor.

King followed the path of the bill with great interest, and his presence in many of the Senate hearings throughout its existence bound the two together. King met with President Johnson a number of times as the bill inched towards completion. Such a realisation enabled King to begin to focus his attention elsewhere: specifically, the need to improve the lives of the USA's poorest people and his opposition to the Vietnam War.

By 1968, the efforts of Martin Luther King Jr. and the Civil Rights Movement were finally starting to affect the country where it mattered: in government. Three years earlier, the movement had helped usher in the first true legislative change for all citizens regardless of colour – the Voting Rights Act, which finally provided lawful rights for African Americans. Now, King and his compatriots had their eyes on the biggest prize of all: amending the Civil Rights Act of 1964.

Despite so many years at the head of the Civil Rights Movement, and legislative change very much a reality for African Americans across the country, King was still leading the charge on all fronts. In 1968, he was organising the 'Poor People's Campaign', which aimed to address the serious economic deficit that alienated poorer areas of society. More importantly, it was a multicultural cause. King was determined to address the poor living conditions of all Americans, regardless of ethnicity.

On 28 March, King made his first major push of the campaign, directing his attention not towards Washington, DC as he had in the past, but towards Memphis and the ongoing Memphis Sanitation Strike. The strike – which saw 1,300 black workers walk out due to dangerous working conditions, discrimination and the horrific deaths of two workers – was national news, and King was determined to use Memphis as a catalyst to kick-start the campaign.

However, an unusual burst of riots and violent incidents brought the campaign considerable negative press, with high-ranking civil rights activist Bayard Rustin even pulling out of the campaign because he felt it was too broad and unrealistic in it s goals of demanding widespread economic rejuvenation.

On 3 April, King flew into Memphis proper in order to make a speech at the Mason Temple (the world headquarters of the Church of God in Christ) – his flight was initially delayed due to a bomb threat, but he made it in time to make the address.

The speech, 'I've Been To The Mountaintop', became one of King's most iconic and well-known orations. "Somewhere I read of the freedom of assembly," he declared. "Somewhere I read of the freedom of speech. Somewhere I read of the freedom of press. Somewhere I read that the greatness of America is the right to protest for rights. And so just as I say, we aren't going to let dogs or water hoses turn us around. We aren't going to let any injunction turn us around. We are going on."

ENEMIES OF THE KING

You don't become a figurehead of the Civil Rights Movement, nonviolent or otherwise, without making some influential foes

J. Edgar Hoover

When it comes to counting your enemies, having the radical director of the FBI as one of them is a feat in and unto itself. While it's not been proven that Hoover had any objection to King's objectives in the Civil Rights Movement, he did attempt to destabilise its progress upon discovering communist spies among his top advisers.

Governor George Wallace

When George Wallace took the Oath of Office for the governorship of Alabama, he brought with him an iron desire to enforce and maintain racial segregation. It was a stance he pursued for many years, especially in spite of King's movements, but he would recant his views in later life.

Malcolm X

While Malcolm X and Martin Luther King Jr. weren't enemies as individuals, their beliefs on how to achieve equality for African Americans were, for a certain amount of time, polarised in the extreme. In his early years, Malcolm X struggled with King's staunch stance of nonviolence, believing that equality could only be achieved through force.

Stokely Carmichael

Once upon a time, a young Stokely Carmichael was a devoted and passionate supporter of King's SNCC, but like many young adopters, he eventually became frustrated with the slow progress of the movement. He would go on to coin and promote the term 'black power' – a phrase King would describe as "an unfortunate choice of words."

Omali Yeshitela

Much like Malcolm X, Yeshitela (born Joseph Waller) rejected King's ideas of racial integration, instead believing that the US (as well as the wider world) could only prosper under black supremacy and a new African nation. He continued to be active in violent protests and, unlike Malcolm X, he never rescinded those supremacist views.

4 April 1968

THE ASSASSINATION

From a simple stroll onto a motel balcony to the flight of an unsuspecting assassin, we break down the murder of a civil rights icon

Memphis, TENNESSEE

By April 1968, Martin Luther King Jr. and the Civil Rights Movement had achieved many of their goals – the Civil Rights Act had been signed into law a mere two days earlier and the Housing Bill Act, which protected the homes of all citizens, was coming into effect. Equality was fast becoming a reality, broadcast across the airwaves of every TV and radio around the world, and King remained the triumphant face of peaceful activism in defiance of age-old tensions and domestic uncertainty. And so, with victory all but certain, King travelled to Memphis for his last push to the mountaintop.

1 15:30
Earlier in the day, ex-convict James Earl Ray had used local news reports and newspapers to determine where King would be staying. At about 3.30pm, he rents room 5B in the run-down Bessie Brewster boarding house, situated across the street from the Lorraine Motel. Ray then heads out and purchases a pair of binoculars for $41.55 from a local store, and returns to the room to watch from his vantage point at the boarding house. He uses a spot in the communal bathroom as a sniping position and waits for King to appear.

2 17:30
It's a balmy evening in Memphis Tennessee and Martin Luther King Jr., key members of his entourage and a large contingent of the movement are staying in the birthplace of rock and roll following King's delivery of the iconic 'I've Been To The Mountaintop' speech at the Mason Temple the day before. King is staying at the Lorraine Motel, a two-storey building on Mulberry Street in downtown Memphis. A popular choice for King when staying in Bluff City, he has just finished getting ready for a dinner with local minister Billy Kyles.

3 18:01
Booked into room 306, King has just finished shaving (he's running late due to an animated conversation with minister Kyles). A group of civil rights members (James Bevel, Chauncey Eskridge, Jesse Jackson, Hosea Williams, Andrew Young and the driver Solomon Jones Jr) are waiting out front in a white Cadillac. Wiping away the shaving powder, King steps out onto the balcony. A single shot rings out; it strikes King through the cheek. Kyles is halfway down the stairs outside when he hears the shot and rushes back to King's room.

4 18:01
With his single shot striking true, James Earl Ray begins preparing to leave. He places his high-velocity rifle, binoculars, a small radio and a newspaper into a box and wraps it in an old green blanket. Mulberry Street and the surrounding area has already descended into chaos. The shot was loud and everyone knows King is staying across the street. Ray places the bundled box outside the Canipe's Amusement Store next to the boarding house. He quickly walks to his nearby car, a white Mustang, and drives away as police arrive.

THE WEAPON

Within a few minutes of the shot being fired on that fateful evening in 1968, Memphis police found a Remington 760 'Gamemaster' (a high-velocity rifle), several unspent rounds and a number of other effects wrapped up in a bundle. Interestingly, the rifle was not found at a vantage point - instead it was discovered abandoned outside the Canipe's Amusement Store across the street from the Lorraine Motel where King was staying. However, FBI and local police reports differ on whether the rifle was actually the one used to kill, with some suggesting the bullet recovered from King's body was incompatible with the purported murder weapon.

Delegate Walter E Fauntroy holds the rifle that was used to kill King

2

3

Y STREET

The red and white wreath at the Lorraine Motel marks the spot where King was assassinated

4

It was from this window, on the first floor of the Betty Brewster boarding house, that James Earl Ray took the shot that killed Martin Luther King Jr

STREET

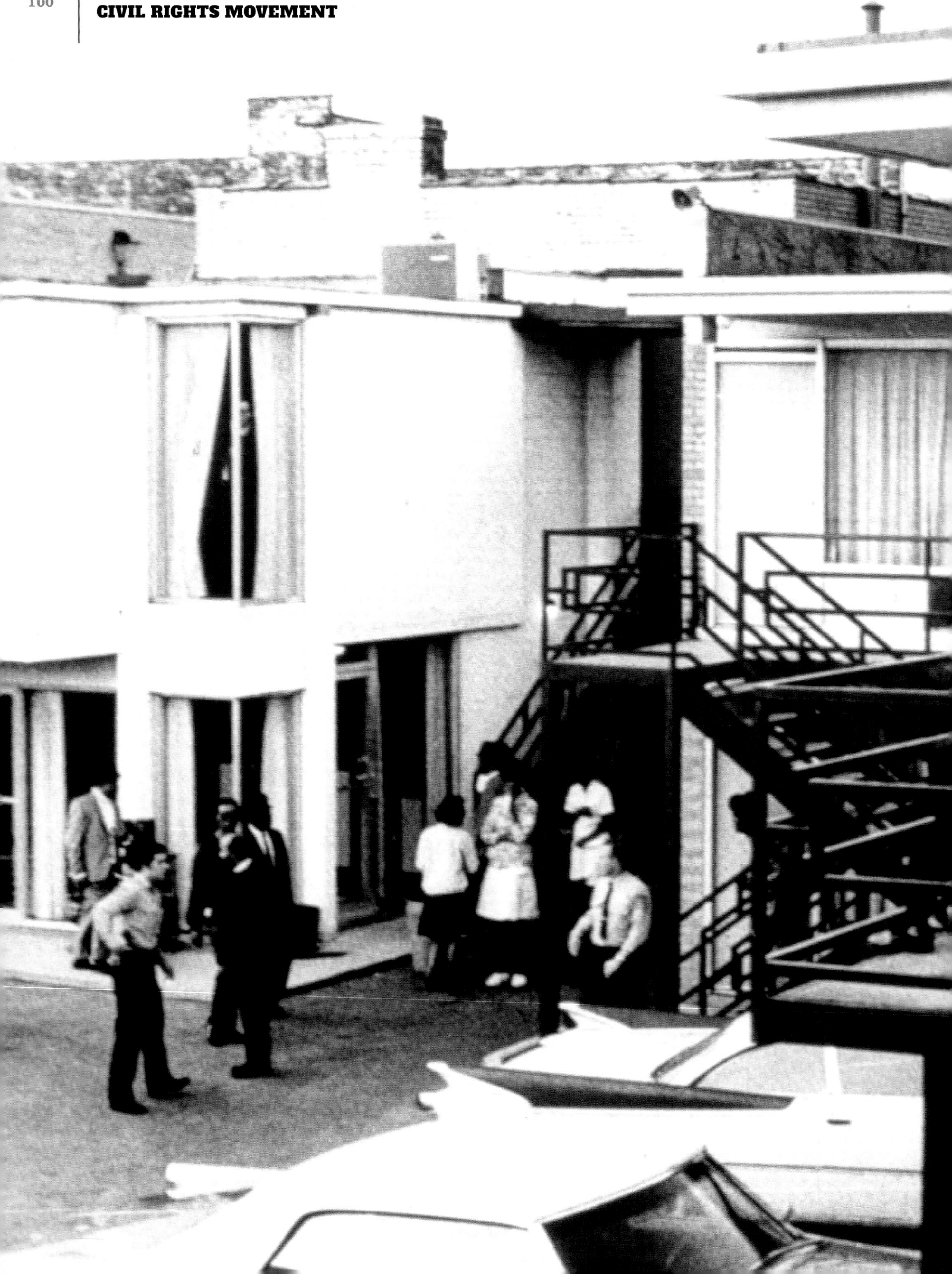

Civil rights leader Andrew Young, left, and others on the balcony of the Lorraine Motel point in the direction of the gunshot. Martin Luther King Jr. lays fatally wounded at their feet

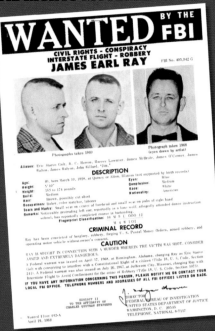

"In the end, we will remember not the words of our enemies, but the silence of our friends"

On 19 July 1968, James Earl Ray is taken to his cell by Sheriff William Morris upon his arrival in Memphis, Tennessee

On 8 April 1968, workers listen to the funeral of Martin Luther King Jr. on a portable radio

WHAT WAS RAY'S MOTIVATION?

1 Ray had racist beliefs

While he was born in Illinois, Ray and his family eventually relocated to Bowling Green, Missouri - a city with a considerable Ku Klux Klan presence. Drawn in by the radical yet influential views of the KKK, Ray reportedly embraced its racist views at a young age - it's these views, tempered by a life of poverty and crime, that may have driven Ray to kill one of the most prominent African Americans in the country's history.

2 He was, and always had been, a poor man

Some believe that one of Ray's motives for the killing may have been purely financial. He'd been born into poverty and had struggled on the breadline for most of his life. Unable to find success in education, Ray's youth and subsequently his adulthood spiralled into a mixture of petty crime and prison spells. There's a possibility that the mysterious 'Raoul' character - who Ray was adamant had hired him to carry out the assassination - could have paid him to take the shot.

3 He wanted the infamy

For most of his life, Ray had lived in inherent obscurity. Born into a life of abject poverty with little aptitude for education, Ray found a sense of twisted purpose and confidence as a criminal. There's a possibility that Ray, knowing the global media attention the death of King would garner, wanted the macabre celebrity status being an assassin would bring.

CONSPIRACY THEORIES

Many remain convinced there's more to the story

The mysterious 'Raoul'

Ray remained adamant he had been hired by a man named Raoul. He had apparently met him in Canada and travelled with him to Memphis to oversee the hit. The FBI dismissed this claim, but in 1998 a retired FBI agent revealed he had found pieces of paper in Ray's car referring to such a suspect.

Lloyd Jowers ordered the hit

One theory doesn't even include Ray as the shooter. It centres on Lloyd Jowers, who ran the Jim's Grill bar across the road from the Lorraine Motel where King was staying. Jowers, in 1993, claimed Memphis produce dealer Frank Liberto paid him $100,000 to hire a hitman - and it wasn't Ray.

It was a government hit

According to Ray's last lawyer, William Pepper, the US government was behind it. In his book, *The Truth Behind The Murder Of Martin Luther King*, Pepper claims a mafia hitman was hired, with the CIA, the FBI and army intelligence all involved in the plot to halt King's influence and frame the unwitting Ray.

After the assassination, demonstrators gather outside the White House

A soldier stands guard in Washington, DC after a building is destroyed by rioters

TRIAL AND AFTERMATH

With the country in a state of shock and national mourning, the attention of the world turned to the man who took the fatal shot

Within moments of unleashing the bullet that would take Martin Luther King Jr's life, James Earl Ray packed his rifle and other effects into a box, wrapped it in an old cloth and fled the boarding house he'd been using to stalk the outspoken minister. Dumping the bundled box outside a nearby amusement arcade, Ray had run to his white Mustang and sped out of Memphis as King lay dying on the first floor of the Lorraine Hotel.

In the days that followed, Ray acquired a Canadian passport under the false name of Ramon George Sneyd and took shelter in the city of Ontario. The FBI issued a warrant for his arrest, adding him to their notorious Most Wanted list while also putting an APB out on all of his known aliases. Two months later, on 8 June, while he was attempting to leave the United Kingdom, check-in staff realised the name Sneyd was on the Royal Canadian Mounted Police watch list. Airport officials also discovered a second passport on Ray under another assumed alias.

Ray was immediately arrested, and extradited to the United States a few days later. In the two months since his flight, the FBI had begun what would, at the time, become the most expensive investigation in the Bureau's history. The manhunt to find Ray had spread across five countries, bolstered by an international outcry at the senseless death of a pro-nonviolence campaigner. Now, with Ray finally in custody, the judicial process could begin.

So what was the case against Ray? Did the authorities have irrefutable evidence of his involvement? In fact, what the prosecution had was purely circumstantial evidence, but all of it placed Ray at the scene of the murder. The rifle used to gun down King bore Ray's fingerprints, as did the binoculars he'd bought earlier that day and a newspaper he had read to gain information on King's whereabouts.

Ray initially confessed to everything to avoid a death sentence, but three days later he withdrew his guilty plea. According to Ray, a mysterious man called 'Raoul' (whom Ray had met in Canada) had orchestrated the entire operation, directing Ray to purchase a rifle and reserve a specific room at the Betty Brewster boarding house. Evidence of such a figure, beyond Ray's own testimony, was never found, and with Ray's troubled history with the law, the prosecution was assured of its confidence in Ray as the killer.

But what had led him into this position? Ever since his teenage years, Ray had been a habitual criminal. Bold but predominantly unsuccessful in his career, his rap sheet was a pockmarked road of armed robberies and thefts. He'd escaped from prison a number of times, including an excursion from Missouri State Prison the year before King was gunned down. Unafraid of wielding a weapon, Ray was described as fearless – but his crimes had never gone as far as murder. A petty thief, undoubtedly, but a killer?

Ray adamantly denied he killed King (a stand he kept until his death in 1998). However, despite the purely circumstantial evidence – including witnesses who identified Ray fleeing the scene – he was convicted of King's murder and sentenced to 99 years in prison.

So why was Ray convicted on such a slim case of evidence? Conspiracy theories continue to run rife as to the inner machinations of the prosecution's case, but one fact was clear: someone had to be made accountable. Five years earlier, the President himself had been gunned down in a similar fashion. Captured on film and immortalised in the minds of all, it left the nation shocked at the simple yet barbaric act of assassination. Much like King, JFK was a popular and charismatic figure and his very public execution galvanised the US into a common desire for justice.

JFK's death was a shocking twist on a Cold War backdrop; King's assassination, however shocking, united the nation in collective mourning. It didn't quell the violence perpetuated by the movement's more radical elements, but it did accelerate the road towards equality. Three months after his death, the Civil Rights Act was signed into law, finally ensuring the constitutional rights of every citizen against unlawful persecution and segregation.

SAY IT LOUD...

21 February 1965

THE ASSASSINATION OF MALCOLM X

Malcolm X's home in Queens, New York, was firebombed just a week before his assassination

When prominent civil rights activist and minister Malcolm Little – better known as Malcolm X – visited the Manhattan Audubon Ballroom to address the Organization of Afro-American Unity, three men from the 400-strong audience stepped forwards and shot him 21 times in the chest. It was a shocking moment, and a public blow to the movement Malcolm X had become so closely associated with, but it was a murder predicated not on race, but religion.

For years, he had spoken publicly about the attempts on his life. In fact, a week before the shooting his home had been firebombed in the night. He knew he was a contentious figure and he embraced his position as a prominent advocate for pan-Africanism and an end to racism, despite the dangers it brought. Much of this hate came from members of the Nation of Islam, an organisation that Malcolm X had left following his disillusionment with its anti-white propaganda. Following a pilgrimage to Mecca, he formed the Organization of Afro-American Unity and preached that racist thoughts, not white people as a whole, were the enemy.

And so, during his fateful speech in Manhattan, three members of the Nation of Islam (Norman 3X Butler, Thomas 15X Johnson and Talmadge Hayer) slipped into the crowd armed with a sawn-off shotgun and two automatic pistols. After causing a commotion to draw the attention of Malcolm X's bodyguards, all three men opened fire on the activist. He was pronounced dead shortly after. Hayer was beaten severely by the crowd and all were eventually taken into custody. All three were charged with murder and sentenced to life in prison in March 1966. The reaction to his death caused outrage, mainly due to the brutality of the act, but a number of detractors were quick to recall he was once a violent activist himself.

Once an angry young activist, Malcolm X soon embraced a far more peaceful outlook on the need for equality in the United States

• The Watts riots
11 August 1965
When an African American motorist was pulled over by police on suspicion of reckless driving, a fight soon broke out between the man's family and the officers. News of the incident spread, and within hours the area of Watts, Los Angeles had descended into riots and looting. A total of 34 died and almost 3,500 arrests were made.

• Stokely Carmichael transforms the SNCC
May 1966
When Carmichael became chairman of the SNCC (Student Nonviolent Coordinating Committee), he used his position to further a cause that had, as yet, failed to get much mainstream attention: Black Power. Carmichael believed nonviolence was a tactic rather than a core principle, which ultimately saw him distanced from other civil rights activists such as Martin Luther King Jr.

• Black Panther Party founded
15 October 1966
Before it spread in popularity across the world (with chapters appearing as far as the UK and Algeria), the Black Panthers were formed to be an armed civilian force tasked with monitoring the Oakland Police Department and its reports of brutality against African American citizens. Considered both revolutionary and deeply socialist, the group operated for almost 20 years.

DEFINING MOMENTS
1965-1968

ORIGINS

The Hinton Johnson incident
26 April 1957

Nation of Islam threatens X
February 1964

Civil Rights Act comes into effect
2 July 1964

LEGACY

Voting Rights Act becomes law
6 August 1965

Martin Luther King Jr. assassinated
4 April 1968

Fair Housing Act
11 April 1968

• Thurgood Marshall appointed to Supreme Court
13 June 1967

This day in the summer of 1967 was a landmark for the American judicial system, as Thurgood Marshall became the first African American to be appointed to the Supreme Court in its long history. Appointed by President Lyndon B. Johnson, Thurgood had held close ties with the NAACP, serving as its chief legal counsel for decades.

• Civil Rights Act 1968
11 April 1968

Often referred to as the Fair Housing Act, this update of the Civil Rights Act was designed to expand upon the principles of the 14th and 15th Amendments, thus strengthening the protections given to racial minorities in matters of housing, renting and equity rights. It's considered one of the most significant victories of the Civil Rights Movement.

• Black Power Olympic salute
16 October 1968

When African American athletes Tommie Smith and John Carlos won gold and bronze medals at the 1968 Olympic Games in Mexico City, the press weren't reporting on the success of their performance, but at the gesture they both made on the podium. With gloved fists raised in the air, the two men showed public solidarity with the Black Power movement at a globally televised event.

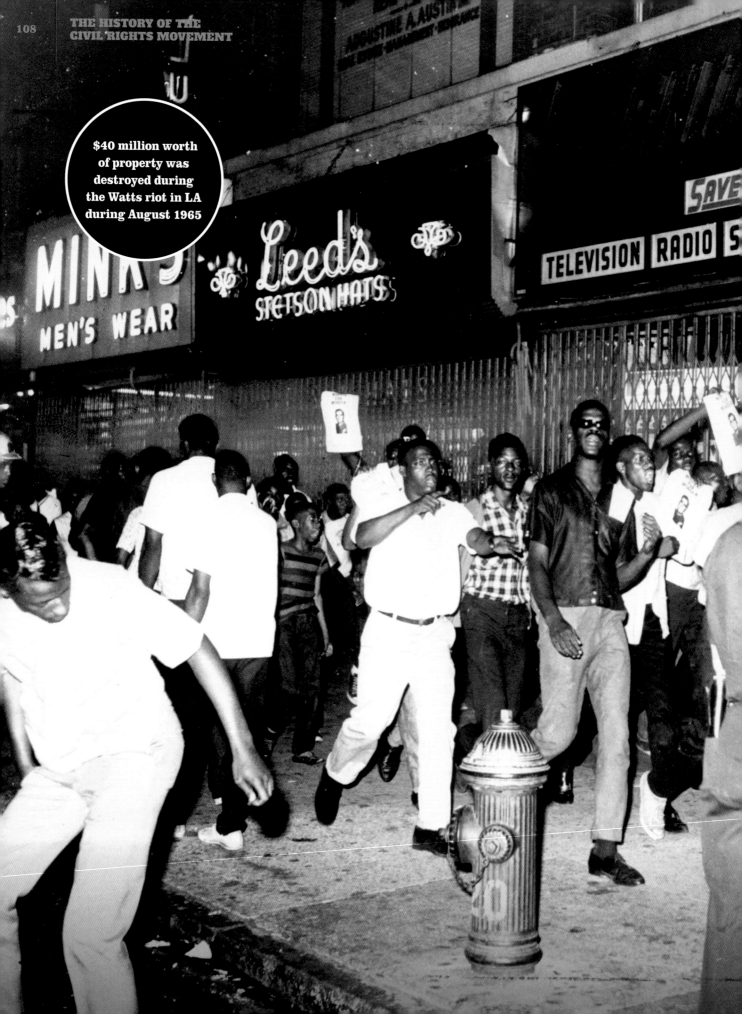

$40 million worth of property was destroyed during the Watts riot in LA during August 1965

A CHANGING MOOD:

RIOTS & REBELLION

The passing of the Civil Rights Act did not bring an end to racial tension. During the mid-to-late 1960s, a disenfranchised youth became ever more angry, sparking riots across the country

The insurgent Civil Rights Movement of the early 1960s brought an end to segregation and boosted black enfranchisement, scoring codified victories with the Civil Rights Act of 1964 and the Voting Rights Act in the following year. Although clearly a step in the right direction, to many black Americans these victories seemed somewhat hollow, "even illusory," according to one prominent scholar.

In spite of the new laws, for African Americans in the North and the West of the country in particular, there had been little real change. Much of the migration out of the South in the preceding decades had been inspired by wartime jobs and these were now in steep decline. The industry that remained, meanwhile, relocated to suburban areas, as did many middle-class whites. The urban centres they vacated evolved into black ghettos that lacked investment, good schools and effective public services.

In addition, police and fire services in these areas remained almost exclusively populated by whites, and many towns and cities organised their policing on containment rather than control policies, turning a blind eye to crime in black urban centres as long as it did not spill into white residential zones. For all the success of the Civil Rights Movement, most young blacks still faced an economically bleak future, and unrest in urban areas continued to simmer.

Then, from 1964 onwards, that unrest began boiling up into violence. One of the first major outbreaks erupted in the Harlem neighbourhood of New York City before mushrooming into six days of violence that spread into nearby Bedford-Stuyvesant. Around 8,000 rioters took to the streets. One person was killed, 118 were injured and 465 were arrested.

Race riots were nothing new in the US, though prior to the 1960s a white population had usually started them as they battled racial integration. A race riot in Memphis, Tennessee back in 1866, for example, was one of the sparks for the formation of the Ku Klux Klan. Of course, some pre-1960 unrest was initiated by blacks, most notably the Harlem riots of 1935 and 1942, both of which erupted under allegations of police brutality. It was the same story in Harlem in 1964, with rioting breaking out after Lt Thomas Gilligan shot dead 15-year-old James Powell.

"A riot is the language of the unheard," said Martin Luther King Jr. "And what is it that America has failed to hear? It has failed to hear that the promises of freedom and justice have not been met. And it has failed to hear that large segments of white society are more concerned about tranquillity and the status quo than about justice, equality, and humanity."

People turned to rioting when other political avenues were closed off, and violent unrest blighted the urban landscape over the next few years. Rochester, Jersey City and Philadelphia were hit in the following months

> **In the Detroit riot of 1967, 9,000 National Guards, 800 Michigan state police, and nearly 5,000 paratroopers were deployed**

before civic violence swept the nation from 1965 onwards.

In August 1965, trouble began in the Watts district of Los Angeles after a police patrol stopped black motorist Marquette Frye on suspicion of driving under the influence of alcohol. Frye was told to step out of the car and, as two armed officers tussled with the suspect, an angry crowd gathered. They soon exploded in a spontaneous burst of anger.

As had been the case with the New York neighbourhood of Harlem the previous year, the residents of Watts had for a long time felt disadvantaged. They mistrusted the white police force, which acted with violent impunity; they lacked jobs, services and education opportunities, while families were forced to crowd together in rundown apartments.

The Marquette Frye incident was the final straw and his arrest sparked five days of rioting, looting, and burning, as the protestors ranged over a 130-square-kilometre section of South Central Los Angeles. They looted shops, burned buildings to the ground and attacked whites. Snipers fired at police officers and firemen from windows and rooftops.

The trouble only came to a close on 16 August after the governor of California mobilised the National Guard. When the smoke cleared, 34

Mayor Jerome Cavanagh called in the National Guard in a bid to contain the Detroit rioters

DETROIT: A CITY ROCKED

On a stretch of 12th Street in Detroit (now named Rosa Parks Boulevard), the raiding of an African American drinking haunt by city police on the night of 23 July 1967, sparked arguably the most infamous riot in American history.

The neighbourhood was typical of the city's rapidly changing geography in the aftermath of World War II, as middle-class whites and Jews rapidly started to relocate to the northwest of the city and black families took their place. The area had a number of 'blind pigs'; drinking joints that served black communities, and a bar owned by William Scott had long been a target for police raids.

Racial tension in the city was already running high. In June, a black Vietnam veteran was shot, while on 1 July, a black prostitute was shot dead, the suspect of an off-duty white police officer. When the police raided William Scott's blind pig on 23 July, breaking up a party held in honour of another black Vietnam vet, a group of local residents gathered to protest the arrests. As the police forced the protestors back, violence broke out and local businesses were looted and cars set aflame.

For a city already on edge, this was a spark in a tinderbox, and rioting flared across the metropolis. Police and fire services were overwhelmed as rioters pelted them with bricks and stones. The city's mayor called for the National Guard. The riot raged for five days, resulting in 7,200 arrests and 1,200 people injured. Forty-three people died, 33 of whom were black.

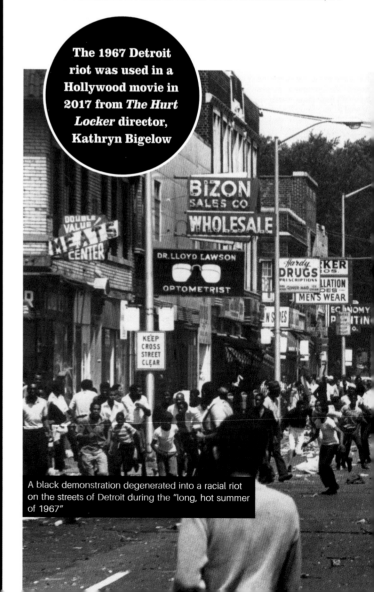

> **The 1967 Detroit riot was used in a Hollywood movie in 2017 from *The Hurt Locker* director, Kathryn Bigelow**

A black demonstration degenerated into a racial riot on the streets of Detroit during the "long, hot summer of 1967"

people had died, 1,032 had been injured and nearly 4,000 had been arrested.

The Watts riots were the worst American urban riots in 20 years and foreshadowed what was to come; racial tensions hit a critical point during what became known as the "long, hot summer of 1967". During that crucial year, when peace-loving students enjoyed their 'summer of love' on the West Coast, race riots gripped almost 160 cities across the country. The most destructive unrest unfolded in Newark, New Jersey, and perhaps most infamously, Detroit, Michigan (see 'Detroit: A city rocked' boxout). Even smaller cities like Cambridge and Maryland were beset by turmoil.

In Newark, tensions flared when a black taxi driver, John Smith, was pulled over by police who beat him up in front of onlookers from a nearby housing project. As with many city police forces, the Newark cops had a reputation among the black population for the use of excessive force. And when a false rumour began circulating that the officers had killed Smith, a large crowd assembled outside the police station.

Many were advocating peaceful protest, though unrest soon rippled through the crowd, which began to hurl bricks and petrol bombs at the police station. Before long a full-scale riot had spread through the dis-

> ## "Race riots gripped almost 160 cities across the United States"

THE KERNER REPORT

At the end of July, President Lyndon B. Johnson ordered a commission to investigate the cause of the 1967 riots and to identify what could be done to prevent another outbreak of violence. The findings were published in March 1968 in a document known as the Kerner Report and stated in bold terms that: "white racism is responsible for the explosive mixture which has been accumulating in our cities since the end of World War II".

The report went on to identify widespread discrimination and segregation in employment, education, and housing, which led to the formation of black ghettos. "Discrimination and segregation have long permeated much of American life," it read. "They now threaten the future of every American.

President Johnson set up a commission to investigate the 1967 riots

"Segregation and poverty have created in the racial ghetto a destructive environment totally unknown to most white Americans," it added. "Our nation is moving toward two societies, one black, one white — separate and unequal," it said. All was not lost, however. "This deepening racial division is not inevitable," it claimed before identifying a number of recommendations "for initiatives and experiments that can change the system of failure and frustration that now dominates the ghetto". The report was widely praised, though the Holy Week Uprising exploded before the major reforms could be put in place.

trict, heralding five days of looting, arson and racial violence. As with Watts in 1965, the National Guard was called in and 26 people were killed. More than 700 were injured and there were more than 1,000 arrests.

If local authorities thought the unrest of 1967 was the apex of civil strife, they were sorely mistaken. The following year saw even more instances of unrest as a wave of public disturbances crashed over the country in the wake of the assassination of Martin Luther King Jr. His murder on 4 April 1968, prompted what has become known as the Holy Week Uprising, the most widespread outburst of social unrest since the Civil War, with large-scale riots in Washington, DC, Baltimore, Chicago, Kansas City, Detroit, New York, Pittsburgh and Cincinnati among others.

In total, cities in 36 states and the District of Columbia experienced looting, arson, or sniper fire. Fifty-four cities suffered at least $100,000 in property damage. More than 58,000 National Guardsmen and army troops joined local state and police forces in trying to contain the violence that saw over 40 people lose their lives, around 2,600 injured, and more than 21,000 arrested. Though more cities suffered, there were actually fewer deaths than during the 1967 riots, with federal and state law enforcers better prepared for rioters, and also under strict orders not to gun down looters.

It was against this background of turmoil in the late 1960s that the Black Power movement gained momentum. Martin Luther King Jr. had been the prime advocate for peaceful resistance and nonviolent protest, and with his death many disillusioned African Americans came to believe that violent resistance was now the only way forward, prompting a surge of support for the likes of the Black Panthers, who espoused separatist ideals and took up arms against the state. By the close of 1968 King's dream had, for so many disillusioned youths, now turned sour.

THE MAKING OF
MALCOLM X

The political activist who challenged the conventions of race and religion amid the chaos of the Civil Rights Movement

Born Malcolm Little on 19 May 1925, the man who would inspire generations first opened his eyes in a city already famed for its perpetual racial tensions. Omaha, the largest city in the state of Nebraska, had a history of clashes between black and white citizens dating as far back as the 1840s, and as the city grew, so did the issue. Omaha had its own chapter of the NAACP (National Association for the Advancement of Colored People) and was home to the Hamitic League Of The World, an African American nationalist movement. The city, and the state as a whole, also had ties to the Ku Klux Klan. It was a hotbed of racial aggression, and Malcolm's family was right in the heart of it.

His father, Earle Little, was an outspoken member of the African American community, a man who wasn't afraid to express his opinions on the strife of his ethnic brothers and sisters. As a local leader of the Universal Negro Improvement Association he wore his beliefs on his sleeve, and it was a mindset that permeated his entire family. As such a prominent figure in the black community, Earle regularly clashed with many white members of the local community – including members of the Klan. So defiant was Malcolm's father in the face of adversity that the Klan once even threatened to murder his entire family. The Littles had no choice but to flee, and little Malcolm was whisked off to a new life in Lansing, Michigan.

Their new life was far from peaceful, though, with Earle clashing with the Black Legion, a KKK splinter group famed for its ultra-violence toward ethnic minorities. In 1929 the Little family home was burnt to the ground; the family escaped relatively unscathed, but Earle was sure the Legion was behind it. Just two years later, Earle was run over and killed by a streetcar in Lansing. The official police report states it was an accident, but Malcolm's mother is convinced her husband was murdered. It's a belief that would stay with her for her entire life, and one that would eventually contribute to her deteriorating mental health. To a young Malcolm Little it was a stark education in the realities of living as a coloured person in the early decades of the 20th century.

In the years that followed, the Littles continued to live through the segregation and second-class citizenship of the times. Without Earle's commanding presence the family sank back into obscurity, with Malcolm and his brothers forced to hunt for game in the surrounding woodland to survive. It was a tough life for any child, but Malcolm, now in his teens, was fast becoming a young man with little fear of anything. The family managed to get by, but tragedy struck yet again in 1937 when his mother Louise was committed to a mental institution. This event shattered the already splintering Little clan.

When one teacher remarked that his aspirations to become a lawyer

Life in the time of
Malcolm X

Rights for Students
In 1951, black students and members of the NAACP began protesting over the continued segregation between white and black children and young adult in schools, colleges and universities around the country. After four years of legal battles, the US Supreme Court ruled that segregation had "a detrimental effect upon the colored children".

Montgomery Bus Boycott
Nine months after a 15-year-old African American student refused to give up her seat to a white passenger, civil rights activist Rosa Parks also made the same statement. She was arrested and charged with civil disobedience, which led her fellow activists (including minister Martin Luther King Jr) to boycott the use of local buses in Montgomery, Alabama.

Desegregation in Little Rock
In September 1957, the small town of Little Rock, Arkansas, was all over the news. Nine African American students who had sued for the right to attend an integrated school found none other than the National Guard waiting to prevent their entry into the school. Ordered there by the governor of Arkansas, Orval Faubus, it took the intervention of President Eisenhower to force Faubus to stand down.

Riding to Freedom
One of the most significant activist statements of the Civil Rights Movement were the Freedom Rides. Conducted in 1961, the event consisted of white and black activists travelling on interstate buses to challenge the continued – and more importantly unconstitutional – segregation on public buses in the Deep South.

Civil Rights Act of 1964
After years of protests, demonstrations and legal action, the wheels for sociopolitical change were finally turning by the mid-1960s. President John F. Kennedy had initially made attempts to push through such legislation prior to his assassination, but was blockaded by filibuster-threatening senators. His successor, Lyndon B. Johnson, eventually forced it through and signed it into law on 2 July 1964.

President Lyndon B. Johnson signing the Civil Rights Act - a piece of legislation that changed North America forever

After returning from his pilgrimage to Mecca, Malcolm X also took the name El-Hajj Malik El-Shabazz

"Despite his excellent grades, Malcolm felt he had no chance of succeeding in a world controlled by white men"

Marked bullet holes in the wall at the site where Malcolm X was killed, during his address to the Organization of Afro-American Unity

At the age of 20, Malcolm X was convicted of larceny and sentenced to prison

THE CIVIL RIGHTS MOVEMENT

In the years Malcolm X was forming his thoughts and beliefs on a pilgrimage to Mecca, his fellow African Americans back in the United States were on the precipice of a social and political revolution. Ever since Abraham Lincoln's Emancipation Proclamation in 1863, black Americans had earned their freedom but the lasting, enabling importance of basic civil rights still eluded them. The Civil Rights Movement, which ran from 1954 to 1968, would change the very fabric of American society forever.

For almost 100 years, African Americans were technically free, but treated as second-class citizens, with segregation between blacks and whites so common it filtered everywhere from schools to restaurants and cafes. The frustrations of an entire people formed the fire of the Civil Rights Movement, a collective with the sole aim of ending segregation and ensuring civil rights for all American citizens in constitutional law. It began with a mixture of nonviolent protests and bouts of civil disobedience, as well as the semi-militarisation of the North Carolina chapter of the NAACP (National Association for the Advancement of Colored People) that protected African American families in the South.

The Civil Rights Movement had many famous faces, including Martin Luther King Jr., Rosa Parks, Andrew Goodman and Malcolm X himself. Many of them gave their lives in the pursuit of their freedoms, with their efforts leading to the Civil Rights Act of 1964 and the Voting Rights Act of 1965.

were "no realistic goals for a nigger", he soon dropped out of high school. Despite his excellent grades, Malcolm felt he had no chance of succeeding in a world controlled by white men. With little keeping him in Lansing anymore, Malcolm slowly drifted into a life of petty crime and soon after became involved in drug dealing, racketeering, theft and more. He lost himself in the simple acts of power, the crimes getting constantly more audacious and dangerous. Eventually the number of thefts caught up to them and Malcolm was arrested and sentenced to eight to ten years in prison for larceny.

Left raw and angry by his experiences as a child and a young man, the future civil rights leader was at a crossroads. While serving time he discovered the teachings of Elijah Muhammad, the leader of a new religious movement, the Nation of Islam (NOI). Its central pillars of paying homage to their African routes and building a community tempered by black self-reliance inspired Malcolm to convert. In 1950, the same year the FBI opened a file on Malcolm, he shed his surname and adopted the letter 'X'. This was used to symbolise the unknown slaves who were ripped from the heart of Africa.

Upon his release from prison in 1952, Malcolm travelled to Chicago to meet with the NOI's leader in person. During his incarceration, he had become an outspoken new member, and Elijah was curious to meet this fearless young firebrand. Impressed with his intelligence and tenacity, Muhammad swiftly promoted him to assistant minister. Now with more influence and standing within the movement, the FBI increased its surveillance of Malcolm, shifting its focus from possible communist ties to his rapid ascent in the NOI. However, to his fellow members he was a breath of fresh air; a man not afraid to look racists in the eye and denounce their arbitrary views.

The Nation of Islam had now become infamous for its radical views. Its ministers preached that black people were the first people of the world, superior in every way to whites. While civil rights organisations fought to destroy segregation, the NOI actively sought it. Malcolm X was now a regular face in the public eye following the Johnson Hinton incident. When the police assaulted Hinton, a black Muslim, Malcolm led a 2,000-strong crowd to the police station to demand he receive medical attention; when the demands

Defining moment
Malcolm's father killed 1931
Aged six, a young Malcolm Little enrols at Pleasant Grove Elementary School in Michigan. That same year, his father is killed after being struck by a speeding streetcar. The official report states it was an accident, but Malcolm's mother Louise is convinced it was murder. His father had been an outspoken leader of the local Universal Negro Improvement Association (UNIA), so rumours run rife that members of the Black Legion had organised a hit on Earle to get rid of a black pride activist. His father had taken out life insurance before his murder but the money is never paid out to the family.

● **Converts to Nation of Islam**
During the early years of his sentence, Malcolm becomes aware of the Nation of Islam, a religious movement originating in the US. He converts and finds inspiration from the words of their leader, Elijah Muhammad. **1947**

Timeline

1931

1947

1952

1925
● **Malcolm X born**
Born Malcolm Little at University Hospital in Omaha, Nebraska, he is the fourth of seven children. His father, Earle Little, is a Baptist lay speaker, while his mother, Louise Norton Little, is a stay-at-home parent. **19 May 1925**

1938
● **Louise Little committed**
After dating a local man for a few months, Louise Little becomes pregnant. The man then vanishes once he learns of the pregnancy, causing her to have a nervous breakdown. She's committed to State Mental Hospital in Kalamazoo, Michigan. **1938-1939**

1943
● **Avoids military service**
At the age of 18, Malcolm moves to New York. He's drafted to the US Army, but is deemed unsuitable for service. Rumours claim he feigned a mental condition to avoid being drafted into service during WWII. **1943**

1946
● **Serving time**
After getting involved in the criminal underworld, Malcolm commits a number of burglaries in and around Boston in 1945. In 1946 he's convicted of larceny (unlawful taking of another's property) and is sent to Charlestown State Prison, Boston. **1946**

1953
● **Preaching across the US**
Elijah Muhammad elevates Malcolm X to the influential position of Minister and sends him to preach at a number of newly opened temples. Over the next two years he spreads the NOI word in Boston, New York and Philadelphia. **1953-1955**

were met, upon a word from Malcolm the crowd left peacefully. It was a sign of his growing power and he used his increased media profile to openly denounce other civil rights movements for their message of protest through nonviolence, stating: "I am for violence if non-violence means we continue postponing a solution to the American black man's problem just to avoid violence". Malcolm's ethos of "by any means necessary" made him an imposing and inflammatory figure to white Americans and those in the African American community who disagreed with him.

After describing the assassination of President John F. Kennedy as a sign of white America's "chickens coming home to roost", the NOI suspended Malcolm, keen to distance itself from the national outcry his publicised words had caused. NOI leader Elijah Muhammad had also grown anxious over Malcolm's popularity in the organisation, fearing his own candidacy would soon be challenged. Soon after, Malcolm announced he was leaving the movement.

After leaving the Nation, Malcolm gave his infamous 'The Ballot Or The Bullet' speech, in which he stressed the need for African Americans to exercise their right to vote and seek full equality. While Malcolm did urge members of the black community to "take arms", he was not urging his brothers and sisters to attack white people. He felt the government was not actively protecting his people from attacks, and so believed they should arm themselves and defend their lives until the government was willing to acknowledge the problem and protect them. During this time Malcolm converted to Sunni Islam, the largest and most common branch of Islam.

A month later, in April 1964, Malcolm left the US on a pilgrimage to Mecca. While there he had an epiphany: he had finally seen the Islamic faith for what it was. Not an armour with which to cocoon one's self in, but a means of bringing the people of the world together. It was the biggest transformation in Malcolm's mind-set since his conversion to the NOI in prison, but it would also prove to be the one that sealed his fate.

Upon his return to the United States, Malcolm had become a sworn enemy of the NOI. While his desire to see the equality and constitutional safety of African Americans was still the central goal that drove him, his beliefs in

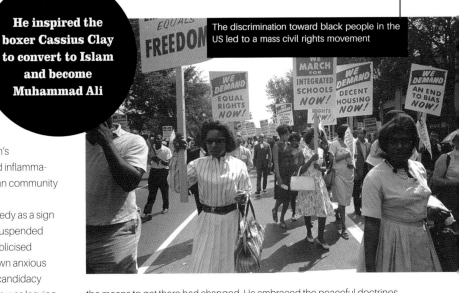

He inspired the boxer Cassius Clay to convert to Islam and become Muhammad Ali

The discrimination toward black people in the US led to a mass civil rights movement

the means to get there had changed. He embraced the peaceful doctrines of Sunni Islam and preached the importance of all Americans, regardless of race, religion or background, working together to achieve equality. For the next 12 months, Malcolm, his wife Betty and his six daughters lived a life under constant threat, but they all knew the importance of pressing forward.

By the beginning of 1965, Malcolm's wife had even contacted the FBI directly, telling them that her husband was "as good as dead" following his refusal to back down in the face of the Nation's death threats. Despite the dangers, Malcolm still campaigned tirelessly, conducting speeches and rallies across the country. On 21 February 1965, Malcolm addressed the Organization of Afro-American Unity at the Audubon Ballroom in New York. Suddenly, someone in the 400-strong crowd shouted, "Nigga, get your hands out of my pocket!" Malcolm and his bodyguards waded into the crowd to quell the disturbance as three men opened fire on him with a sawn-off shotgun and automatic pistols. Malcolm was struck 21 times and was pronounced dead shortly later.

He may have been prematurely removed from the world, but Malcolm X made an impact that's still felt today. While his views were often controversial, no one can deny his bravery in fighting against the establishment for much-needed change.

Defining moment
Freedom at last 1952
After serving six years of his eight to ten-year sentence for larceny, Malcolm is released from prison. Having become a dedicated follower of the Nation of Islam, Malcolm soon comes to the attention of Elijah Muhammad. He meets with Muhammad in Chicago and a few weeks later is appointed an assistant Minister for the movement. Around this time he abandons his birth name Little and starts using the surname X. Around this time the FBI also creates a file for him, following a letter he writes to President Truman opposing the Korean War.

Defining moment
Assassinated in Manhattan
21 Feb 1965
Following a pilgrimage to Mecca the year before, Malcolm returns a far less radical man. He begins denouncing any form of violence and urging people of all colours to work together to attain civil rights for all. He receives death threats from a number of more radical Islamic groups, including outspoken members of the Nation of Islam. His wife Betty even contacts the FBI and tells them her husband is "as good as dead." While preparing to address an Organization of African-American Unity rally in Manhattan, Malcolm is shot dead by angry militants. Three men are arrested and sentenced to life in prison.

1965

1957
● **Johnson Hinton incident**
Four members of the Nation of Islam are beaten with nightsticks by New York police officers. After the men are arrested, Malcolm arrives with a crowd of some 4,000 NOI followers and forces the police to give them medical attention. Covered by national news, it is the first time Malcolm permeates the public eye.
26 April 1957

1958
● **Malcolm meets Betty**
In 1955, Malcolm meets Betty Sanders at one of his lectures. A year later she joins the Nation Of Islam and takes the symbolic surname X as the two continue to court. In January 1958 Malcolm proposes over the phone and they marry two days later.
January 1958

1963
● **Courting infamy**
Following the assassination of John F. Kennedy, reporters approached Malcolm X for a comment on the event and he described it as "chickens coming home to roost". The comments cause national outrage and he is barred from representing the Nation of Islam.
1 December 1963

1964
● **Leaving the NOI**
Malcolm splits from the NOI and soon converts to Sunni Islam. He meets Martin Luther King Jr for the first and only time at a Senate debate on the Civil Rights Bill. At this time he also urges African Americans to be prepared to take up arms if their voting rights are not protected.
8 March 1964

BLACK POWER BLACK PANTHERS

Despite the progress made by the Civil Rights Movement, many black Americans still felt disenfranchised, leading to the rise of Black Power groups – most notably the revolutionary Black Panthers

hroughout the 1950s and early 1960s the Civil Rights Movement made huge strides towards racial equality, and yet by the mid 1960s black people across the country still felt excluded from meaningful influence. Millions were debarred from political representation as well as quality education and employment opportunities. A middle-class lifestyle seemed a million miles away. The American Dream was not their reality. Frustrated with the status quo, many turned to 'Black Power'.

This term has a long history, and a variety of definitions, though it took on a very specific meaning when evolving into a public slogan during the March Against Fear in June 1966. James Meredith, the first African American to gain admission to the University of Mississippi and a man Martin Luther King Jr. described as a hero of the Civil Rights Movement, began a solitary march from Memphis, Tennessee, to Jackson, Mississippi, in a bid to encour-

age black American voter registration. Two others marched with him.

On the second day of the march a white sniper called James Aubrey Norvell opened fire and hit Meredith in the shoulder. Outraged, members of the Southern Christian Leadership Conference, the Congress of Racial Equality (CORE), and the Student Nonviolent Coordinating Committee (SNCC) rallied behind Meredith's cause and the likes of King, Stokely Carmichael and Floyd McKissick were joined by hundreds more as they completed the march.

And it was during this march, after he was arrested and held in jail for six hours, that Stokely Carmichael stirred up a crowd in Greenwood, Mississippi, declaring, "We want Black Power!". This was the first time this phrase had been engaged as a public rallying call, its use by Carmichael a battle cry for violent resistance to white oppression. It chimed with many. "When you talk about Black Power you talk about bringing

At the 1968 Olympics, medallists Tommie Smith and John Carlos raised their arms in the Black Power salute

this country to its knees any time it messes with the black man," Carmichael said later.

Initially, the SNCC and CORE had been strong exponents of non-violent resistance, though many of their members felt that the times were changing. And when Carmichael succeeded to the chairmanship of the SNCC prior to the Meredith march, he advocated change. It appears that he had only ever regarded nonviolence as a temporary measure, not a key tenet of his belief. His move towards a call for armed resistance caused King much concern.

King believed that "the slogan was an unwise choice" and he tried to dilute its provocativeness, writing that "the Negro is powerless" and should therefore seek "to amass political and economic power to reach his legitimate goals". Carmichael, however, disagreed, and with both the SNCC and CORE repudiating nonviolence, huge ruptures emerged within the Civil Rights Movement. Like King, organisations such as the Southern Christian Leadership Conference and the National Association for the Advancement of Colored People rejected Black Power and

On the other side, dozens of different organisations sprung up in support of Black Power, though neither Carmichael nor any other Black Power proponents offered a coherent and organised route to achieving its goals. Many young blacks knew that they wanted to mobilise and to fight for their rights but they saw no structured solutions. How would they mobilise? What exactly should they do?

Into this void stepped Huey Newton and Bobby Seale. In October 1966, just four months after the Meredith march and Carmichael's provocative speech, Newton and Seale formed the Black Panther Party for Self-Defense. The pair had come together years earlier in the Revolutionary Action Movement (RAM), a Marxist black organisation vehemently opposed to what it regarded as American imperialism.

It was from RAM that they drew the idea, which was pivotal to Black Panther politics, that black America was a colony within the country, and the struggle against racism was part of the global anti-colonial struggle against imperialism. RAM did not consider black Americans citizens of the US; they were an independent nation that had been colonised on

KEY FIGURES IN THE BLACK POWER MOVEMENT

Huey Newton

The co-founder of the Black Panthers was jailed for killing Officer Frey, his incarceration becoming a rallying call for activists. He was released after three years. As the movement petered out he instead turned to drug use and died during a drug deal in 1989.

Bobby Seale

The co-founder of the Black Panthers, Seale served a four-year prison sentence for inciting a riot in Chicago during 1968 and was tried again in 1970 in a case focused on the torture and murder of fellow Panther, Alex Rackley.

Stokely Carmichael

By the time Stokely Carmichael was elected chairman of the SNCC in May 1966, he advocated violent resistance. He eventually joined the Panthers though he was at loggerheads with other party leaders who sought bonds with anti-imperialist whites.

Eldridge & Kathleen Cleaver

Eldridge Cleaver and his wife Kathleen fled police harassment and set up a Panther branch in Algeria. After falling out with Newton, they went on to form the Revolutionary People's Communication Network.

Robert F. Williams

Williams' book, *Negroes with Guns*, detailed his experience with violent racism and his disagreement with the nonviolent wing of the Civil Rights Movement following the attacks visited upon him in Monroe. The text was a big influence on Newton.

Mao Zedong's 1963 essay linked the struggle for black liberation with the war against imperialism

forefront of opposition to the Vietnam War.

RAM's honorary chair-in-exile Robert F. Williams, the author of *Negroes with Guns*, had been a member of the National Association for the Advancement of Colored People, though he took up arms to protect himself from racist violence in Monroe, North Carolina. To escape prosecution, and also a potential lynching, Williams took refuge in Cuba and forged links with Mao Zedong in China.

The group's influence on Newton and Seale was profound, though the two men were aware of the group's limitations. Most members of RAM were intellectuals, rather than practical activists, and they offered few solutions to how their doctrine could mobilise young blacks in America. Newton and Seale eventually severed their ties with RAM and hit upon a way of standing up for their rights.

Throughout 1966 racial tensions were rising in their hometown of Oakland, and in the state of California as a whole. When police shot 16-year-old joyrider Matthew Johnson in San Francisco in September, Newton and Seale decided the situation had become untenable. They would protect their neighbourhoods with patrols. A scheme called the Community Alert Patrol had already emerged in Watts in the aftermath of the infamous 1965 riot, whereby activists would monitor police patrols. They even sported an image of a panther on their vehicles. The vital difference for Newton and

A teacher gets his class to raise their hands in support of Black Power

Black Panther supporters rally outside Alameda County Courthouse as Newton goes back on trial in 1970

> *"A wave of black uprisings crashed across the nation... rebellion re-emerged as an act of political expression"*

Seale, however, was that their patrols would be armed.

During the remainder of 1966 the Black Panthers made several stands against the police, citing local ordinances and the Second Amendment, asserting their rights to carry arms in their vehicles as long as the weapons were not concealed. And yet the group's membership remained quite small. However, all that changed in the following year, in the wake of a number of shootings of black men by police in North Richmond, most notably the suspected murder of Denzil Dowell.

Despite contradictory evidence, a white jury vindicated the officers' actions in the Dowell case and many residents of North Richmond began looking to the Panthers for support, bringing their own weapons to rallies and pledging their allegiance to Newton and Seale. "They had organised the rage of a black community," says one prominent writer on the subject, "into a potent political force".

The Panthers' influence began to spread outside the state of California during the summer of 1967 when in response to earlier incidents between the Panthers and the police, the state legislature introduced a bill seeking to outlaw the carrying of loaded firearms in public. In May, 30 armed and uniformed Panthers arrived at the State Capitol building in Sacramento in order to protest against the bill. A number of them were arrested, and the bill passed, although it proved a PR coup for the Panthers. The press coverage was intense and thousands of young blacks across the country became aware not only of the Panthers, but of their message of armed

In 1969, Stokely Carmichael quit the Panthers and left the US for Guinea, where he worked for pan-African unity

THE SLAYING OF HAMPTON AND CLARK

Chicago in 1969 was simmering with tension. The city's police force waged a campaign against the Panthers and there were numerous reports of police brutality. One Panther, Jake Winters, took a famous stand, shooting dead two officers and injuring eight more before he was gunned down. This was the backdrop to the Fred Hampton attack on 4 December. The Panthers were angry, but the law enforcement agencies wanted revenge; they would step up their operations.

Fred Hampton, ca 1968

The FBI had already planted informant William O'Neal into the Chicago chapter, where he was appointed the Panthers' chief of security, and during November he supplied the Bureau with detailed information about the movements of Chicago chapter leader Fred Hampton. He also provided them with a detailed map of Hampton's apartment. At 4.30am on 4 December, a group of 14 officers gathered outside Hampton's home. They did not carry their usual weapons of intimidation – tear gas and sound equipment – these officers carried a submachine gun, five shotguns, a rifle and several high-calibre handguns. They had a very specific mission in mind.

Their assault was executed with precision. By 4.45am Hampton lay dead in his bed, shot twice in the head, once in the arm and shoulder. He was 21 years old. Fellow Panther leader Mark Clark, 17, was also killed. Seven other Panthers in the apartment - four of whom carried bullet wounds - were arrested on charges of attempted murder, aggravated battery and unlawful use of weapons.

And yet, according to the findings of the federal grand jury, 90 bullets were fired inside the apartment of which one came from a Panther. *The New York Times* visited the apartment and noted that while the areas where the dead Panthers had slept were clustered with bullet holes and shotgun gouges, "There were no bullet marks in the area of the two doors through which the police said they entered". In spite of all the evidence, no officers were ever charged with the murders of Hampton and Clark. O'Neal received a $300 bonus.

resistance. By the end of May 1967, the Panthers had a keen membership dedicated to revolutionary ideals.

And then came the 'long, hot summer' of 1967. A wave of black uprisings crashed across the nation and for the first time since the urban revolts during World War II, rebellion re-emerged as an act of political expression. There were many different groups espousing Black Power, though it was the Black Panthers that moved to place themselves in the vanguard.

The Panthers' first moves were cautious, historians noting that when the party published its ten-point programme in the second issue of *The Black Panther* newspaper at the start of the summer, it seemed as though it was trying to explain itself, using language that lacked the confidence that should have been commensurate with its expanding influence nationwide. Yet as rioting spread the Panthers' confidence started to grow. One of the new recruits was Eldridge Cleaver, a writer and key figure in the Black Power movement who had played a role in recruiting the Panthers as armed bodyguards for Malcolm X's widow, Betty Shabazz, early in the group's formation.

Cleaver became an important member of the party and in its nascent years used his connections to forge alliances with other left-leaning and Black Power groups. It was Newton, though, the Panthers' minister of defence, who was the key player. As the Panthers' influence spread it was Newton who members regarded as the true leader. It is hardly surprising then, that when Newton was arrested on suspicion of the murder of Officer John Frey on 28 October, his release became the party's primary focus.

The 'Free Huey!' campaign attracted more press attention and when the police responded with brutal ferocity against protesters during October 1967's 'Stop the Draft Week', many leftists took up the campaign, seeing it as yet another way to protest against American imperialism. In early 1968, the party's influence really began to blossom when the Panthers announced a merger with the SNCC. And then, a few months later, everything changed.

The assassination of Martin Luther King Jr. in April 1968 saw another conflagration of racial violence ravage the country. Two days later, during a shootout between Panthers and cops in Oakland, an unarmed 17 year old, the Panthers' national treasurer Lil' Bobby Hutton, was gunned down. The political establishment went on to appropriate King as a martyr for American democracy, but the Panthers now had Hutton as their own martyr and tens of thousands of young black Americans mobilised in support of the party's cause. White support grew, too; Marlon Brando was one of the mourners at Hutton's funeral. Newton, meanwhile, was cast in the role of a political prisoner, incarcerated for his radical views.

By the December of 1968, the party had grown to such a size that it had offices in 20 cities all across the country. With Newton directing proceedings from his jail cell, the party also developed an intelligent strategy towards armed struggle. They remained an overt operation and did not direct their members to go on the offensive against the police. However, by stating that their members should arm themselves and should fire on any law enforcers seeking to enter their homes without a warrant, they were creating the conditions that could lead to firefights. By the end of the year, the Panthers had emerged as the most powerful black movement in the country.

The Panthers used their growing influence to help their communities and in January 1969, began the first of their Free Breakfast for School Children programmes at St Augustine's Church in Oakland. By the end of the year, the Panthers had set up kitchens in cities across the nation, feeding over 10,000 children every day before they went to school.

The government was concerned. As early as August 1967, the FBI launched COINTELPRO, a programme designed to neutralise what the Bureau described as "black nationalist hate groups". In September 1968, as more and more Panther chapters opened across America, FBI director J. Edgar Hoover dubbed the Black Panthers "the greatest threat to the internal security of the country". Over the next few years the federal government and local police forces launched a concerted attack on the Panthers, regularly feeding defamatory stories to the press, wire-tapping offices and recruiting informers.

"The Panthers had set up kitchens in cities across the nation, feeding over 10,000 children every day"

A toddler and party members giving a Black Panther salute

The Black Panther headquarters in Harlem circa 1970

The Black Panther Party for Self-Defense shortened its name to the Black Panther Party in 1968

MOVE ON OVER OR WE'LL MOVE ON OVER YOU

Early Black Panthers poster, circa 1966

View of protesters gathered for an 'Avenge Fred Hampton' rally, held at Boston Common, 1970

The American far-left, anti-racist, White Panther Party formed in 1968, in response to a call from Newton

View of a line of Black Panther Party members as they stand outside the New York City courthouse

The FBI tried to create rifts within the party, leading to internal violence and deaths, and it appointed agent provocateurs in a bid to encourage the Panthers into large-scale public attacks. They even sought to undermine the breakfast programme. On occasion, they simply attacked Panther chapters, shooting up the offices and making multiple arrests. Aggression against the Panthers saw the emergence of the first SWAT team, wearing flak jackets and assault rifles. Sometimes, officers gunned down Panthers in cold blood, Fred Hampton is a case in point (see 'The slaying of Hampton and Clark' boxout).

One of the FBI's key moves was to incite tension between the Panthers and the black nationalist group Organization Us, which culminated in the shooting of Panther captain Bunchy Carter and deputy minister John Huggins on the UCLA campus in January 1969. Another firefight between the two groups in March resulted in the deaths of two more Panthers. It's ironic that state repression and agitation only boosted party membership. By the end of 1970 almost 70 different cities had Panther chapters.

For all the FBI's efforts, it was internal as well as external forces that initiated the Panthers' decline. A broader membership over an ever-expanding geographical area made it more difficult for the party to enforce its rules. The Panthers were forced into a number of purges and there are some shocking examples of in-group torture and murder – such as that perpetrated against Alex Rackley – as the group sought to identify and oust informants. Inter-party altercations and dissent began to increase, some of which was fostered by the FBI.

Yet arguably the greatest obstacle to the Panthers' continued rise was the slate of concessions introduced by the government throughout 1970.

President Nixon scaled back the draft and the anti-war sentiment gained further mainstream support. Black people began to enjoy more social access and political representation, while the overseas governments that had forged links with the Panthers entered into discussion with the US government. The party was quickly beginning to lose its raison d'etre.

By the time Newton travelled to China in September 1971, the Black Panther Party had started to disintegrate, though it would remain active for many years to come. By mid 1972 it had contracted to become a local Oakland organisation once more. A slow and often undignified demise followed before the Panthers finally closed their final office in 1982.

★ ★ ★

Tanks and soldiers funnel
marchers during the Memphis
Sanitation Strike in March
1968. Martin Luther King Jr.
would travel to Memphis to
support strikers before being
assassinated on 4 April 1968.

LEGACY

/ISION ON A 'DAILY

SE WORDCAS

LIVES MATTER

USTICE FOR
TRAYVON!
& BYRON CARTER

CLEVELAND

The 1963 March on Washington brought the Civil Rights Movement a tremendous amount of media exposure and raised the national consciousness

CIVIL RIGHTS: ACHIEVEMENT & ANGUISH

The Civil Rights Movement has made great strides towards equality for blacks in American society, but the complete delivery of the promise remains elusive

The Holt Street Baptist Church in Montgomery, Alabama, was crowded. Not a seat was available as 27-year-old Dr. Martin Luther King Jr. stepped to the pulpit to deliver a galvanising oration. King preached peace and nonviolent change, and he warned, "We are here this evening to say to those who have mistreated us so long that we are tired... tired of being segregated and humiliated, tired of being kicked about by the brutal feet of oppression."

Four days earlier, Rosa Parks, a secretary in the local office of the National Association for the Advancement of Colored People (NAACP), had been arrested for refusing to give up her seat on a Montgomery city bus to a white man and move to the back of the vehicle, where black citizens were – by law – obliged to find room. Others had been arrested and jailed for the same 'offence,' but Parks' ordeal and Dr. King's speech during those pivotal days are generally remembered as the beginning of the Civil Rights Movement.

To be sure, black Americans had organised previously. The NAACP had been in existence since 1909, and other groups such as the Congress of Racial Equality (CORE) and the Student Nonviolent Coordinating Committee (SNCC) had also come into being, contributing to the tapestry of the growing Civil Rights Movement. Despite the pervasiveness of Jim Crow; the insidious Black Codes, that undid the promises of the 14th and 15th Amendments to the US Constitution, guaranteeing equal protection under the law and voting rights for blacks; and the US Supreme Court's odious affirmation of the doctrine of "separate but equal" in the Plessy v Ferguson decision of 1896, progress had been made. In 1948, President Harry S. Truman had desegregated the US Armed Forces and mandated equal opportunity for all in the military. In 1954, the Supreme Court had established the intent, though sluggish at best, to implement the desegregation of public schools across the country with its decision in Brown v the Board of Education of Topeka, Kansas.

It was in Montgomery, however, that the national consciousness of blacks was raised to the status worthy of being called a 'movement.' The ensuing year-long boycott of the city's public transportation system and its 1956 victory in US District Court in the Browder v Gayle case against both city and state-endorsed segregation on public transportation – a decision upheld by the US Supreme Court – gave impetus for the continuation of the burgeoning movement under the leadership of young Dr. King.

More than half a century after its beginning in 1955 through to its peak in the late 1960s, and with acknowledgment to the continuing influence of its legacy, an assessment of the achievements of the Civil Rights Movement yields moments of triumph, frustration and tragedy. Without question, the Civil Rights Movement succeeded in drawing the focus of the nation to the inequities and social injustice that were present, particularly in the South. King's personal magnetism drew followers and supporters, both black and white. With the immediacy of television, Americans witnessed the struggle for equality against police wielding clubs, fire hoses, vicious dogs, bombings, demonstrations, and murders. Like any effort to affect tremendous social change, the movement brought the best and the worst of human interaction to the forefront, and it made a difference in the world as it is today.

In terms of accomplishments, by 1957 President Dwight D Eisenhower was compelled to enforce Brown v the Board of Education when nine black children enrolled for classes at the previously all-white Central High School in Little Rock, Arkansas. When Governor Orval Faubus defied the federal government, Eisenhower sent troops of the 101st Airborne Division to escort the children into the school. King and his Southern Christian Leadership Conference were inspiring a generation of activists to nonviolent protest, and Eisenhower signed the Civil Rights Act of 1957, the first federal civil rights legislation signed by the executive branch of the government since Reconstruction. A cabal of powerful Southern congressmen succeeded in reducing the scope of the legislation, and in the eyes of many observers the measure was in reality more symbol than substance. Nevertheless, the Civil Rights Act of 1957 established the Civil Rights Division of the Justice De-

When Dr. King set up the SCLC, he said "We must... conduct our struggle on the... plane of dignity and discipline"

partment and enabled the federal government to prosecute anyone accused of denying or curbing the rights of another citizen to cast a vote in any election. A six-person Civil Rights Commission was also empanelled with the responsibility for investigating infringement of voting rights. By far, though, its greatest impact was the confirmation of the expanding commitment of the federal government to the advancement of civil rights.

In 1960, the SNCC was sponsoring sit-ins at lunch counters where blacks were forbidden to receive service. A series of sit-ins in Greensboro, North Carolina, caused the F.W. Woolworth Company, with stores across the nation, to end its racial segregation policy in the South. A year later, CORE organised the Freedom Rides, and activists rode buses from Washington, DC, to New Orleans, Louisiana, to call attention to the segregation still prevalent in bus terminals, waiting areas, rest rooms, and other gathering places. The Freedom Riders, originally seven blacks and six whites, were threatened, harassed, and physically assaulted. One bus was firebombed. The violence escalated in Montgomery to such a level that US Attorney General Robert F. Kennedy was compelled to send 600 federal marshals to the city to quell the disturbance and protect the Freedom Riders. The implication was clear. If federal and state governments were reluctant

SHIRLEY CHISHOLM'S TRAIL

In 1972, New York congresswoman Shirley Chisholm declared herself a candidate for the nomination of the Democratic Party as president of the United States. Thirty-seven years later, Barack Obama was sworn in as the nation's 44th president.

Chisholm was the first woman to aspire to the Democratic nomination, the first black woman to do so, and also the first black individual to seek the highest office in the land. Therefore, President Obama owes a debt of gratitude to Shirley Chisholm, a trailblazer in party politics, gender, and racial equality, and the opportunity was facilitated during the political awakening of the Civil Rights Movement.

Born in New York City in 1924, Chisholm was the child of Caribbean immigrants. A 1952 graduate of Teachers College of Columbia University, she worked as an educator before running for the New York State Assembly in 1965. In 1968, she was elected to the US House of Representatives from the state's 12th District, becoming the first black woman elected to Congress. Although her bid for the presidential nomination was unsuccessful, Chisholm did receive 430,703 votes, or 2.69 per cent of the ballots cast in the democratic primary. She finished seventh among 15 hopefuls, opening the door for minority candidates of the future. Chisholm died at the age of 80 in 2005.

New York Congresswoman Shirley Chisholm was a pioneer in American politics and sought the Democratic Party's nomination for president

> " *A series of sit-ins in Greensboro... caused the F.W. Woolworth Company... to end its racial segregation policy in the South* "

A massive throng jams the National Mall in Washington, DC, during the Million Man March in 1995

to enforce the measure enacted by the Supreme Court, then passive, nonviolent resistance would force them to act.

During the historic March on Washington in 1963, a crowd estimated at 250,000 or more gathered on the National Mall, and Dr. King delivered his impassioned – and now immortal – 'I Have A Dream' speech on the steps of the Lincoln Memorial. His emotive call for an end to racial segregation and injustice was catapulted by television, radio, and newspapers into the homes of millions of Americans. An estimated 30 per cent of those in attendance at the March on Washington were white, evidencing an awakening of civil rights fervour that transcended black consciousness alone. The Civil Rights Movement had succeeded in becoming a focal point of the most turbulent period in American history since the Civil War.

Even so, it was not until the following summer, the so-called 'Freedom Summer', that many Americans, shocked at the brutality of the opposition to the Civil Rights Movement, were spurred into action. The Ku Klux Klan (KKK), a violently racist and segregationist hate group, was alive and well in the South and elsewhere in the United States and took horrific action against an initiative to register voters in Mississippi. Despite laws that supposedly had put to rest the methods that whites

The bus where Rosa Parks was arrested is now a museum exhibit in Montgomery, Alabama

---

> In March 1960, JFK prohibited discrimination of race, religion, or national origin in federal government hiring

ANYONE FOR TENNIS?

Harvard-educated Ralph Bunche was one of the first black Americans to serve as a prominent representative of the US government. In 1945, he participated in the formation of the United Nations and the drafting of its landmark Universal Declaration of Human Rights. During the early days of the nation of Israel, Bunche was a leading negotiator with Arab and Israeli representatives. For his efforts, he received the Nobel Peace Prize in 1950. Bunche participated in the Civil Rights Movement, attending the March on Washington in 1963 and the Selma to Montgomery March two years later.

After receiving the substantial Nobel Prize monetary award, Bunche purchased a home in the Kew Gardens area of Queens, New York, where he lived from 1953 until his death 28 years later. In 1959, Bunche and his son, Ralph Jr, applied for membership at the Westside Tennis Club in Forest Hills, New York. They were denied on the basis of race. After a media frenzy, the official who had led the effort against their membership resigned. The club officially apologised and later offered Bunche a membership, but he declined, refusing to accept solely on the basis of his personal prestige and the publicity of the experience.

had used to suppress the black vote under Jim Crow, few real gains had been made in the number of black voters going to the polls as the Black Codes were slowly being strangled.

Three college students, white New Yorkers Michael Schwerner and Andrew Goodman, and James Chaney, a black worker from Meridian, Mississippi, were abducted and murdered. The perpetrators of the heinous crimes included white men who were prominent local officials and citizens, law enforcement officers, and ardent members of the KKK. Although the murders of three innocent young men may hardly be seen as an achievement, the sheer cruelty and ruthlessness of the incident engendered a groundswell of support for the Civil Rights Movement. The opinions of many of those who had previously been indifferent to what was happening to other people, were changed forever.

The murders also hastened Congressional approval of the landmark Civil Rights Act of 1964, signed into law by President Lyndon B. Johnson. Among other prominent components, the act made equal access for all to public facilities – including restaurants, sports arenas, theatres, and parks – the law of the land. Further, in regard to the glacial pace of public school desegregation, the federal government was empowered to file lawsuits against states, municipalities or districts that refused to comply with the Supreme Court's 1954 decision. Most famously, the act prohibits discrimination on the basis of race, colour, religion, sex, or national origin.

A year later, President Johnson signed the Voting Rights Act of 1965, which provided sweeping governmental powers to assure that the right of any American citizen to vote would not be impeded. Subsequently amended five times to broaden its scope, the act is considered one of the most effective modern measures ever approved by Congress. The act prohibits the requirement that an individual submit to a "test or device" in order to vote, including literacy tests, attainment of a certain level of education, or proof of good moral character.

Ralph Bunche was a highly respected diplomat and recipient of the Nobel Peace Prize in 1950

States and jurisdictions that endeavoured to change voting laws were made subject to the review and oversight of the federal government.

Even as the Civil Rights Movement reached the zenith of its power and influence, with the support of the federal government in its advocacy for change, the movement itself experienced something of an identity crisis. Factionalism crept into its leadership and became more prominent. Although a united front had been presented during the days of the Montgomery Bus Boycott, a decade later some elements of the movement were becoming restless and dissatisfied with the pace of reform. They questioned the value of continued passive, nonviolent resistance. More militant voices were heard. Malcolm X, a Muslim minister and one of the most influential orators of the era, called for more forceful action, pan-African unity, and separation of the races rather than integration. Detractors asserted that he preached his own brand of violence and racism. After repudiating his former affiliation with the militant Nation of Islam, he was assassinated by three members of the organisation in New York on 21 February 1965.

In the autumn of 1966, activists Bobby Seale and Huey Newton founded the Black Panther Party, far to the political left and embracing tenets of Marxism and socialism. The Black Panthers initially formed to monitor police activities in the city of Oakland, California, and expanded to include chapters in major American cities as well as abroad. Although some activists rallied to its views on the struggle to end the oppression of blacks, the organisation became involved in illegal activities and its popularity eroded considerably by the early 1980s. Racially and reactionary motivated violence, marked by loss of life and the destruction of property, erupted from time to time. In August 1965, a series of riots broke out in the Watts neighbourhood of

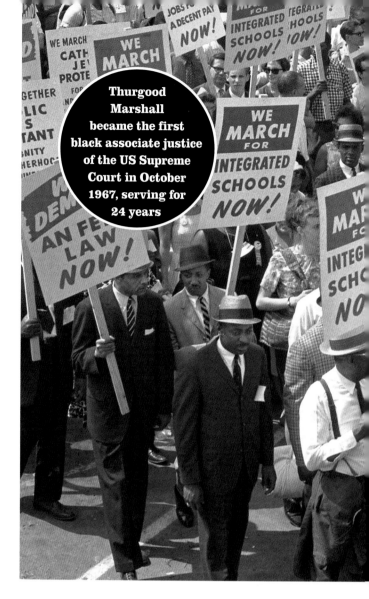

Thurgood Marshall became the first black associate justice of the US Supreme Court in October 1967, serving for 24 years

INTERRACIAL MARRIAGE PROHIBITION

In the years following the Civil War, one statute that was common across America prohibited the intermarrying of the races. In 1887, several states, including Pennsylvania, Illinois, Ohio, and Michigan, repealed laws against interracial marriage. Between 1948 and 1967, numerous states, including much of the West, repealed their laws. Among these states were California, Oregon, Colorado and Nebraska.

On 12 June 1967, the US Supreme Court handed down a unanimous decision in the case of Loving v Virginia, stating that the prohibition of interracial marriage was unconstitutional. With the decision, laws against such unions in every state of the Deep and Mid South were voided, as were laws in West Virginia and Missouri. The case had been brought by Mildred and Richard Loving, a black woman and white man married in Washington, DC, in June 1958. Returning to their Virginia home, they were charged with violating Section 20-58 of the state code. After pleading guilty to "cohabitating as man and wife against the peace and dignity of the Commonwealth," they were sentenced to a year in prison.

The sentence was suspended on the condition that the Lovings leave Virginia. They relocated to the District of Columbia and filed suit. A marked increase in interracial marriages followed the Supreme Court decision.

Mildred and Richard Loving brought the landmark suit against the state of Virginia that overturned statutes prohibiting interracial marriage

Civil rights supporters carry signs and take to the streets during the March on Washington for Jobs and Freedom, 28 August 1963 in Washington, DC

Los Angeles, California. The violence stemmed from police detaining a motorist on a possible reckless driving charge and quickly escalated amid accusations of police brutality. Thirty-four people died, more than 1,000 were injured, and nearly 4,000 arrested. When Dr. King was felled by an assassin's bullet on 4 April 1968, violence broke out in 125 cities across the United States. After King's death, his heirs assumed the mantle of their martyred leader, building upon his legacy of peaceful resistance and asking Americans to search their collective souls to make the country a more tolerant place to exist.

One of the prime movers in the developing factionalism within the Civil Rights Movement was the obvious lack of progress in social and economic equality. While equal access to education, housing, jobs, healthcare, and the attainment of the elusive 'American Dream' might be legislated and advocated in theory, the reality was that systemic, often covert racism persisted and lingers to this day. Bodies of law such as Affirmative Action, a by-product of the Civil Rights Movement, have been enacted to provide opportunities for black Americans and other minorities. Just days after Dr. King's assassination, early legislation was passed by Congress to address equal access to housing. Blacks have faced historic discrimination in such common activities as borrowing money, purchasing homes in areas of suburban America, merit-based promotion and advancement in the workplace, and acceptance in professional and managerial roles.

As the Civil Rights Movement succeeded in calling attention to the endemic racism in the US, it also blazed a trail for other disadvantaged groups, including Asian and Hispanic minorities, women, gays, lesbians, and others. Each of these has made significant strides in the wake of the Civil Rights Movement. Despite resistance, the movement, as far as the gains that were within its grasp, must be considered a success. Still, its reach was limited. Real change that results in a better society for all has to begin with the individual. A changed perspective on the world cannot be legislated into existence.

Such is the challenge that continues to loom, prompting the Reverend Jesse Jackson to stand once again on the National Mall in 1995 and address the huge crowd during the Million Man March. "Why do we march?" he asked. "Because our babies die earlier. Why do we march? Because we're less able to get a primary or secondary education. Why do we march? Because the media stereotypes us. We are projected as less intelligent than we are, less hard working than we work, less universal than we are, less patriotic than we are, and more violent than we are... Because we're trapped with second-class schools and first-class jails."

The Civil Rights Movement served an important purpose, succeeding admirably where possible and perhaps providing a springboard to a new society, one of opportunity and mutual support among all Americans.

Obama drew the largest ever crowd for a presidential inauguration in 2008 with nearly 2 million people

BARACK OBAMA:
THE WATERSHED PRESIDENT

How the political career and presidential victory of an African American proved one of the Civil Rights Movement's most significant legacies

ack in 2009, the British Broadcasting Corporation unearthed footage of an interview conducted with iconic Civil Rights Movement leader, Martin Luther King Jr. Recorded in 1964, four years before his assassination in Memphis, the interview made headlines because it showed King making the most remark-

40 years," he claimed in response to a similar suggestion from former Attorney General Robert Kennedy. "I would think in 25 years or less."

And so, it would seem fitting that 45 years later an African American would campaign his way to the Oval Office. When Barack Hussein Obama was sworn into office as the 44th president of the United States on 20 January 2009, he not only brought a true sense of diversity to the most powerful political position in the world, but fulfilled one of the dreams of the Civil Rights Movement's most prominent figureheads.

Obama's success as a Democratic candidate for the presidency was a watershed moment for the United States. It was the culmination of a changing political, social and economic landscape, one fundamentally shaped by the efforts and bloody victories of the Civil Rights Movement throughout the 20th century. The criminalisation of racial discrimination in 1964; the right for black people to vote in 1965; Thurgood Marshall becoming the first black associate justice of the Supreme Court of the United States in 1967; the right to fair housing in 1968. For all its bloodshed and instilled racial division, America was evolving on multiple levels.

When the Democratic Party nominated Obama for the presidential race in 2008, the United States senator for Illinois found himself in a perfect storm of political components. Born in Hawaii to a white mother and black father, Obama embraced his mixed heritage yet comfortably identified himself as a man of colour. His race was a part of him, but not the factor that defined him. His unflappable manner, impressive oratory skills and background as a civil rights attorney in Chicago helped build a persona very few opponents could use against him.

The DNA of America's political arena was also transforming in the late 2000s, a factor that became all too apparent when the presidential election kicked off in late 2008. For years, the country had often voted in the same manner, states often locked into stiff political allegiances. The electorate of the Northeast and West Coast were almost always Democrat blue while the majority of the rest of the nation voted Republican red. But not in 2008. Something was shifting and the prospect for a black president was becoming a favourable choice.

By 4 November 2008, Obama emerged victorious in a hard-fought race with Republican candidate and US military veteran John McCain. With 52.9% of the votes, his victory might seem a close-run affair, but Obama's campaign took not only the popular vote (with 69,498,516 voting for Obama), but the electoral vote as well (claiming 365 votes to McCain's 173). It was an impressive victory, indicative of a nation that wanted out of the Iraq War and a renewed focus on domestic healthcare and economic reconstruction.

Despite the unmovable South and the states of the 'Old Confederacy' voting for McCain, Obama's campaign won decisive victories in the Northeast (including key political battlegrounds such as Ohio), winning the hotly contested vote in New Mexico and Iowa, and gaining vital sup- port in the long red-only South (with Florida, North Carolina and Virginia all voting Democrat).

And so an African American man would become the 44th president of the United States. Ultimately, Obama's skin colour wasn't the reason he was elected to office, but it didn't prevent him from doing so either.

However, despite this huge step towards true racial equality America has taken with the election and re-election of its first black president, there's still a long way to go. Racial tensions have risen to their highest in half a century and the United States has become the anchor point of a new, modern Civil Rights Movement – one fighting injustices all too famil- iar to those that fought so hard for equality in the past 100 years or more.

OBAMA'S ROOTS IN CIVIL RIGHTS

Long before the idea of running for any kind of political office had entered Barack Obama's mind, the young future president pursued a career in law in his home state of Illinois. He became a visiting fellow, then a lecturer and finally senior lecturer from 1991 to 2004 at the University of Chicago Law School, all the while becoming heavily involved in civil rights cases across the state. It was also here that Obama began his campaign for healthcare improvements.

In 1992, Obama took over the orchestration of Illinois's state-wide Project Vote programme, a campaign designed to deal with the stag- gering 400,000 unregistered African American voters living in the state. It was a mammoth task, but it still managed to hit its target of registering 150,000 black voters. In fact, the feat was so impressive it led *Crain's Chicago Business* (a local business-focused newspaper) to name Obama as one of its '40 under Forty' individuals to watch in 1993. He was also involved in a number of high profile cases, includ- ing Buycks-Roberson v Citibank Fed Sav Bank, which claimed the financial institution had condoned practices that undermined the Fair Housing Act (a cornerstone of the Civil Rights Movement).

After a decade-long career in law, Obama would go on to become a state senator in Illinois for seven years

Obama is a devout Christian, and can be seen here attending the African Methodist Episcopal Church in Washington, DC

BIRTH OF THE NEW CIVIL RIGHTS MOVEMENT

Black Lives Matter has sparked the spirit of protest against the racism faced by African Americans and black people across the globe. The new struggle mixes civil rights and the politics of Black Power

Trayvon Martin was only 17 when he was killed walking back from the shops. His killer, George Zimmerman, followed him because he looked 'suspicious', provoked a confrontation and then shot the unarmed teenager to death. But police had to be pressured into arresting him, weeks after the event, because they believed he acted in self-defence. The eventual trial stirred all the stereotypes of the 'black super human menace', and Zimmerman was ultimately acquitted. On hearing the verdict, activist Alicia Garza wrote a Facebook post in dismay, which ended with the words "Our Lives Mat-

ter". Her friend Patrisse Cullors took this phrase and created the hashtag #BlackLivesMatter, which spread as quickly as the pain from the verdict. The killing of an unarmed black teenager ignited the spirit of protest not for the first or last time in American history.

Emmett Till had a profound impact on the Civil Rights Movement without ever marching, protesting or making a speech. As a 14 year old visiting family in Mississippi, he was lynched by a racist mob for 'disrespecting' a white woman. His mother, Mamie Till, insisted the mutilated body of her child was displayed in an open casket at the funeral. The

image sent shivers down the collective spine of America and galvanised support for the Civil Rights Movement. It is a sad testament to just how little has changed that 60 years later it was the killing of a black teenager that awoke the masses.

#BlackLivesMatter was sparked by the killing of Trayvon Martin but found its platform when unarmed teenager Michael Brown was shot dead by a police officer in Ferguson, Missouri on 9 August 2014. Protests erupted in Ferguson, whose population was two-thirds African American, while its police force had only three black officers in total. Michael Brown's killing was the straw that broke the camel's back in police-community relations and major periods of unrest broke out in the city through the remainder of 2014 and into 2015. Stories of police brutality, racism and the targeting of African Americans were a reminder that many of the same problems that existed in the original civil rights struggle persist in contemporary America. The original movement may have outlawed discrimination and segregation, while securing voting rights for African Americans, but it had not guaranteed equality before the law or her officers. Tamir Rice, Eric Garner, Philando Castile and Korryn Gaines represent

just a fraction of those killed by the police that are testament to the most fundamental form of racial injustice.

Since emancipation from slavery, African Americans have been victims of the criminal justice system. One of the ways that free black labour was retained in the South was to put prison chain gangs to work. African Americans were subject to incarceration for fines and minor offences to ensure they would populate the chain gangs. Though being victimised by the prison system is not new; between 1980 and 2012 there was a 222 per cent increase in the incarceration rate in America. The war on crack cocaine was a major factor in this steep rise, and hugely disproportionately put African Americans into prison. Almost a million African Americans spend time in prison each year, and it is estimated that there are more black men behind bars today, or on probation and parole, than there were enslaved in 1850. Mass incarceration has become perhaps the most important civil rights issue in the 21st century. The impact of loss of liberty, voting rights and ability to find employment led Michelle Alexander to declare the prison industry the "new Jim Crow". With around five million African Americans outside of prison under state

Protests over the police shooting of Michael Brown in Ferguson, Missouri

The shooting of Alton Sterling in 2016 led the DOJ to open a civil rights investigation

supervision on a daily basis, the police have become ever-present in black communities. To some they have come to symbolise the boots on the ground of racism, the militarised storm troopers of racial injustice.

Black Lives Matter is similar to the Civil Rights Movement in that it is a banner for a number of independent organisations, which existed before the hashtag came into being. It has grown into an international organisation with 40 chapters around the world. They use the same name and adopt the policy platform but are run by those who were already working on the ground. Just as with the Civil Rights Movement, they offer support and training for activists in an effort to maximise their effectiveness. The movement is a coalition of forces aimed at bringing about social change. In the same way that the Big Six civil rights leaders, which included Martin Luther King Jr., James Farmer and A Philip Randolph, were national spokespeople for the movement, so are figures like Alicia Garza, Patrisse Cullors and Opal Tometi. Leadership is an area where Black Lives Matter tries to distinguish itself from the Civil Rights Movement, as Alicia Garza explained in an interview for The Guardian: "If you're only looking for the straight black man who is a preacher, you're not going to find it."

An enduring criticism of the civil rights struggle is that it was sexist, and focused too narrowly on issues that impacted directly on men. We remember the charismatic male leaders who rallied the troops and set the agenda, and ignore the women who toiled behind the scenes. BLM has rejected this patriarchal idea, started by three gay black women, it has aimed to empower a leaderful organisation that is open to the whole black community. Bayard Rustin is one of the most important civil rights activists but because he was gay, his story is most often overlooked. In contrast, De-Ray Mckesson has become one of the most prominent voices associated with BLM. This is no small difference; civil rights was blighted by its pursuit

"Police are ever-present in black communities"

Students from New York City schools at the second annual Future of the City March against police brutality

A march through Park Lane, London, in 2016, to demonstrate against the killing of black men by police in the US

BLM co-founder Alicia Garza speaking at CitizenUCon16 in March 2016

BLM co-founder Opal Tometi on *The Laura Saunders Show* in August 2015

BLACK LIVES MATTER IN THE UK

One of the notable differences to the Civil Rights Movement is how BLM has spread across the world. The movement has inspired protests in countries such as France and South Africa, as well as becoming a driving force behind black struggle in the UK. In July 2016, following the killings of Alton Sterling and Philando Castile, who was live-streamed bleeding out on Facebook, protests erupted across the UK. Thousands of mainly young people took to the streets in all the major cities protesting in solidarity. BLM UK had been organising before, with the support of the American founders, but the movement gained national attention with these protests. In August 2016, BLM organised civil disobedience, shutting down the tram service in Nottingham, and blocking roads in Birmingham as well as the M4 exit to Heathrow Airport. BLM UK aims to raise the profile of those who have died in custody, or after police contact, in Britain, including Kingsley Burrell, Sarah Reed, Mzee Mohammed and Mark Duggan. Just as in America, black people in the UK are more likely to die under suspicious circumstances after police contact and are actually even more over-represented in the prison population. BLM UK has also broadened the issue from criminal justice to issues such as immigration, poverty and climate justice.

"BLM aims to be leaderless in order to promote a diversity of voices"

of presenting a respectable version of blackness that would be palatable to mainstream America. Mckesson's mantra "I love my blackness, and yours" is the perfect response to the limits of past movements.

BLM aims to be leaderless in order to promote a diversity of voices but also to prevent damage caused by the figurehead being brought down or betraying the cause. Assassinations of figures like Martin Luther King Jr. act as a cautionary tale for investing too much in a leader. Emphasis is placed on being 'leaderful' and empowering activists within different chapters. This is more similar to the organising of the Civil Rights Movement than we have been taught to remember. The figureheads may linger in the memory but the reality is that it was a broad coalition of black activists that made the movement a success. BLM is actually more traditionally led, with a platform, chapters and its own programmes. In contrast, the Civil Rights Movement is a label we have placed over a range of different and sometimes competing ideas and organisations.

Trying to both lead, and be leaderless, puts BLM in a difficult practical position. In the desire to not dictate solutions, they have created BLM as more of a kitemark than an organisation. A badge that sanctions the work of activists on the ground. When asked about the similarities between BLM and the Black Panther Party, former Panther Kathleen Cleaver insisted that they "were not a movement" but an organisation. She stressed

BLM co-founder Patrisse Cullors accepting the Sydney Peace Prize in November 2017

DeRay Mckesson, a voice that has come to the fore in BLM

the clear ideology, structure and programmes of the Panthers, which is something that BLM purposefully lacks on the national level. The national agenda of BLM includes Channel Black, for media representation; a Black Futures Month programme; and a series of high profile "provocateur events". This is a far cry from the Panthers' newspaper; free breakfast programmes; medical clinics; legal advice, as well as strict party discipline being centrally administrated. It should not be a surprise that BLM is more similar to the Civil Rights Movement in terms of scope when the goals are similar: to protest in order to produce policy change. The

Colin Kaepernick (centre) and teammates from the San Francisco 49ers take a knee in protest during the pre-game playing of the national anthem

COLIN KAEPERNICK STARTS NFL NATIONAL ANTHEM PROTESTS

In September 2016, San Francisco 49ers quarterback Colin Kaepernick brought international attention to the issue of police brutality and racism by refusing to stand for the national anthem, which is routinely played before every NFL game. He explained: "I am not going to stand up to show pride in a flag for a country that oppresses black people and people of colour." His protest was inspired by Black Lives Matter and before long, other players joined in by taking a knee during the anthem. The protests proved controversial with NFL owners, many fans and even the US president. In October 2017, President Trump encouraged the NFL to take a zero-tolerance approach to players who "disrespect our flag, our country" and said that he would implore owners to say "get that son of a bitch off the field right now" if they refused to stand during the anthem. The following week over 200 NFL players took a knee. Since July 2017 Kaepernick has been without a team and is suing the NFL for collusion. He has continued his activism and donated $1 million to a range of social justice organisations.

Panthers could take up arms to defend the community from the police, while BLM engages in peaceful protest, because they were not interested in public opinion but revolutionary practice. Both groups gained a high profile by taking up the issues of criminal injustice, and the youth and urgency of BLM has created a connection to the Panthers in the popular imagination. But to really understand BLM we have to go back to a fissure that broke out within civil rights activists.

Younger and more militant activists in the Civil Rights Movement grew tired of the incremental, "overcome them with our capacity for love" approach of King and the leading organisations. Stokely Carmichael (later Kwame Ture), of the Student Nonviolent Coordinating Committee (SNCC) manifested this frustration when he used the term 'Black Power' at a rally in Mississippi in 1966. Black Power was a cry for recognition, to not have to accommodate the interests of white society in order for legislative change. Black Power is often seen as its own distinct movement, a rebuke to the more traditional civil rights leaders. We think of slogans like "Black is beautiful"; the militancy of the Panthers; and Malcolm X's fiery speeches against the "white devils". In doing this we forget that the roots of Black Power were the Civil Rights Movement, young people frustrated by the slowness of change and tone of the struggle.

If social media were around in the 1960s, Black Power would have been a hashtag, a way to capture a range of ideas and feelings and to insist that

Defining moment
Trayvon Martin 26 Feb 2012

Neighbourhood watch volunteer George Zimmerman fatally shoots unarmed 17-year-old Trayvon Martin as he returns from the shops in Sanford, Florida. Following the killing of Martin, rallies, marches and protests take place across the United States. Claiming self-defence, Zimmerman isn't initially charged but increased attention from the media leads to him eventually being tried for Trayvon's murder. However, he is acquitted of second-degree murder and manslaughter in 2013. The killing of Trayvon and Zimmerman's acquittal is widely seen as the spark that led to the creation of the Black Lives Matter movement and its campaigns against violence and systemic racism towards black people in America.

JUSTICE FOR TRAYVON!

CAN'T BREATHE

Timeline

2012

2013
- **Miriam Carey, Washington DC**
  While making a U-turn at a White House checkpoint, Carey hits a police car. Police give chase before shooting her dead. Her 13-month-old daughter is in the back of the car.
  3 Oct 2013

2014
- **Laquan McDonald, Chicago**
  17-year-old McDonald is shot 16 times by a police officer. After a video of the incident is released, numerous protests are held across several months.
  20 Oct 2014

2014
- **Tanisha Anderson, Cleveland**
  Anderson's family call 911 as she is having a mental-health episode. Police arrive and she dies as a result of being restrained on the ground by officers.
  14 Nov 2014

2014
- **Tamir Rice, Cleveland**
  The 12 year old is shot by a police officer as he plays with a toy gun. It is later revealed that the officer was deemed unfit for duty by his previous force.
  22 Nov 2014

2014

2015
- **Walter Scott, North Charleston**
  Unarmed Scott is shot in the back as he attempts to flee from police. The officer claims Scott took his taser but an eyewitness video reveals this not to be true.
  4 April 2015

2015
- **Freddie Gray, Baltimore**
  Gray fell into a coma shortly after being arrested. He died a week later due to injuries to his spinal cord. Protests are held throughout the country.
  19 April 2015

A police officer patrols during a protest in support of BLM in New York on 9 July 2016

Ferguson has faced many protests since the shooting of Michael Brown by a police officer

black life matters. When Malcolm X talked about the need to "elevate the civil rights struggle to the level of human rights", what he meant was that black people were not respected as human beings. The phrase "Black Lives Matter" is the simplest representation of that idea. You cannot legislate our basic recognition as people, and this is where BLM directly embraces the legacy of Black Power and explains the generational divide between BLM and the surviving civil rights royalty.

Open hostility has been displayed towards some of the veterans of the Civil Rights Movement when they have tried to engage in the moment defined by BLM. At a rally in Washington in 2014, organised by Al Sharpton's organisation, BLM activist Johnetta Elzie stormed the stage, upset that the younger activists' work was being co-opted. There is the feeling it is time for a fresh, grassroots approach to the problems and the established way of parachuting figureheads into hotspots has run its course. This split is not a new development and goes back to the debate in the 1960s. The younger activists were inspired by Malcolm X's urgency and bought into being Black Power, but it largely remained in the sphere of civil rights. There are a few examples, like the Panthers, who took up the revolutionary mantle, but in the main the movement aimed to better integrate African Americans into the system. Even cultural activists like Amiri Baraka, who wanted to maintain distinct African American cultural

"There is the feeling it is time for a fresh, grassroots approach to the problems"

communities, did so in tandem with civil rights gains. Baraka started a Committee For a Unified Newark (CFUN) in 1968, an organisation that worked extensively with Newark officials to try to carve out some space in the city for African Americans. This meant supporting electoral candidates and encouraging people to vote, rather than destroying the system.

Black Power became so loosely defined that it was used in calls for better integration into capitalism as well as by those wanting to bring about communism. Black Lives Matter faces the same problem of being too broad a platform. It is almost as impossible to disagree that black life matters, as it is to agree to what the solution is. In taking the coalition for policy reform model, BLM is the 21st century version of the Civil Rights Movement. The question now is whether we need to reinvent the civil rights approach, or abandon its politics for a more radical vision of revolution.

Defining moment
Eric Garner 17 July 2014
Garner is approached by police in New York on the belief that he was illegally selling cigarettes. One officer grabs Garner from behind before putting him in a chokehold or headlock for up to 20 seconds before he loses consciousness. In a video of the incident Garner can be seen yelling "I can't breathe" 11 times. He's pronounced dead at the hospital around an hour later. Garner's cause of death is ruled as compression of the neck. However, on 3 December a grand jury decides not to indict the officer responsible. By the end of the year around 50 protests against police brutality are held across the country.

HANDS UP DONT SHOOT AUG 9, 2014 R.I.P. MICHAEL BROWN

Defining moment
Michael Brown 9 August 2014
A police officer notices Brown fitting the description of a man who reportedly stole cigars from a store close to where they were in Ferguson, Missouri. The officer pulls his car next to Brown. After an altercation the officer shoots an unarmed Brown 12 times, killing him. Peaceful protests are held the day of the shooting but they soon turn violent, starting what is known as the Ferguson Unrest, with the slogan 'Hands Up, Don't Shoot' being widely chanted at demonstrations. No charges were filed against the officer. The killings of Martin, Garner and Brown spark debate across America about the relationship between the police and black Americans, fuelling the Black Lives Matter movement and bringing the issue of violence towards black people into the eyes of the world.

2015
● **Sandra Bland, Waller County**
Bland is found hanged in a jail cell three days after being arrested during a traffic stop. Protesters call for an investigation into the cause of her death.
13 July 2015

2016
● **Alton Sterling, Baton Rouge**
Sterling is shot several times while being held on the ground by two police officers. No charges are filed against the officers involved.
5 July 2016

2016
● **Philando Castile, Falcon Heights**
Seconds after Castile is shot by police, his girlfriend Diamond Reynolds livestreams a video to Facebook of the officers as Castile lays fatally wounded.
6 July 2016

2016
● **Korryn Gaines, Randallstown**
Gaines is shot dead and her five-year-old son wounded during a standoff with police. Gaines records the incident, but Facebook deactivates her account due to a police request.
1 Aug 2016

2016
● **Terence Crutcher, Tulsa**
Crutcher, who is unarmed and has his hands in the air, is shot by a police officer while also being tasered. He dies in hospital later the same day.
16 Sep 2016

2016
● **Keith Lamont Scott, Charlotte**
Lamont is shot by a black police officer, leading to both peaceful and violent protests throughout Charlotte. No charges are filed against the officer.
20 Sep 2016

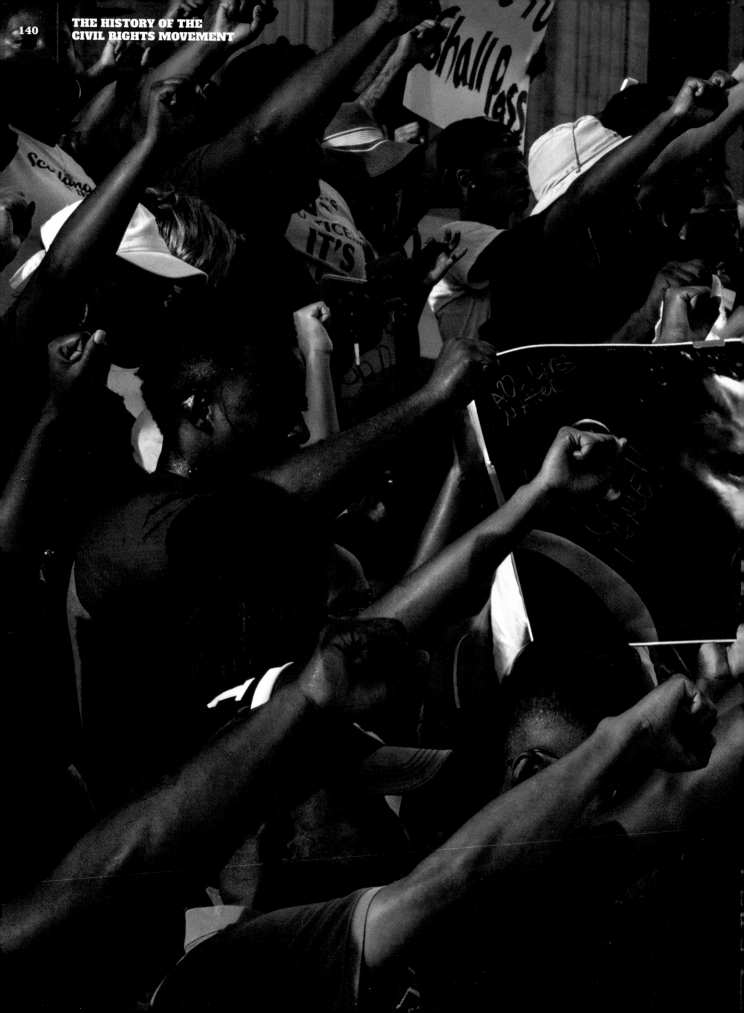

Demonstrators hold up an image of Martin Luther King Jr. and Barack Obama on 9 July 2016 as they protest the shooting of Alton Sterling by a Baton Rouge police officer.